CW00919728

● ║soho
● ║theatre + writers centre

Toby Whithouse

Jump Mr Malinoff, Jump

Winner of the Verity Bargate Award 1998

Soho Theatre is supported by   stone
Arts and Business Pairing Scheme, Foundation for Sports and the Arts
Performances in the Lorenz Auditorium. Registered Charity No: 267234

Cast

in order of appearance

George Malinoff	Paul Chequer
Nick Malinoff	Justin Salinger
Emily Deacon	Laura Sadler
Pasha Malinoff	Robin Soans
Dougie Price	Martin Freeman

Director	Jonathan Lloyd
Designer	Luke Hunt
Lighting Designer	Jason Taylor
Sound Designer	Matt McKenzie
Russian Language Coaches	Barbara Norden
	Nikolai Kozin

Literary Manager	Paul Sirett
Casting Director	Carrie Hilton
Production Manager	Julian Cree
Stage Manager	Nicole Walker
Assistant Stage Manager	Lorna Seymour
Wardrobe Supervisor	Anna Barcock

Press Representation
Bridget Thornborrow Arts Publicity (020 7247 4437)

Advertising
Haymarket Advertising for Guy Chapman Associates

Graphic Design (season)
Unlimited (020 7462 5718)

Images
Stone (www.tonystone.com)

Soho Theatre and Writers' Centre
21 Dean Street, London W1V 6NE

Admin: 020 7287 5060   *Fax:* 020 7287 5061
Box Office: 020 7478 0100
www.sohotheatre.com   *email:* mail@sohotheatre.com

Biographies

Paul Chequer
George Malinoff
Trained at Guildhall School of Music and Drama. Film: Tea with Mussolini; The Low Down. TV: Holby City; As If. Theatre: Billy and the Crab Lady (Soho Theatre); Trade and Bluebird (Royal Court) and A Woman of No Importance (Royal Exchange, Manchester).

Justin Salinger
Nick Malinoff
Trained at Guildhall. Theatre includes The Backroom (Bush) and Perpetua (Birmingham Rep); Peter Pan as Peter (Royal National Theatre); Much Ado About Nothing (Cheek by Jowl); Chips with Everything (RNT); Candide (The Gate); Dona Rosita the Spinster (Almeida); Salome (RNT Studio) and Dealer's Choice (RNT). Television: The Vice; Dark Realm; London's Burning. Film: Peaches and Velvet Goldmine.

Robin Soans
Pasha Malinoff
Theatre includes Hamlet (Young Vic); Moonshine (Plymouth/Hampstead); The Invention of Love; The London Cuckolds; Volpone (all Royal National Theatre); The Country Wife, Venetian Twins, Murder in the Cathedral (all Royal Shakespeare Company); Three Birds; Etta Jenks; Waiting Room Germany; Stargazy Pie and Sauerkraut (all Royal Court); Shopping and F**king (Royal Court/Out of Joint); The Positive Hour (Hampstead/Out of Joint). Films includes Hidden City, Comrades, Blue Juice, Sabotage, A.K.A.

Laura Sadler
Emily Deacon
Theatre includes Lift Off, About The Boy and Blue Bird (all Royal Court); Julie Johnson (London New Writing Festival/The Gate) and Six Characters in Search of An Author (Royal National Theatre). Television includes Anchor Me; Belfry Witches: Grange Hill; Simply the Best; The Fallen Curtain; Anything's Possible and Inspector Morse. Film includes Intimate Relations; Eureka and Coming Home.

Martin Freeman
Dougie Price
Trained at Central School of Speech and Drama. Martin can be seen in the BBC 2 sketch show Bruiser. Other TV includes The Office; Casualty; Lock Stock; The Hello Girls; This Life II and The Bill. Theatre includes Silence (Birmingham Rep); La Dispute and Angela Carter's Cinderella (both Lyric Hammersmith); Woman in Black, Dealing with Clair and A Going Concern (all Stephen Joseph Theatre); Jump to Cow Heaven (Hull Truck); The Wasp Factory

(West Yorkshire Playhouse);
Swamp City (Birmingham Rep
Studio); Mother Courage and
Her Children and Volpone (both
Royal National Theatre). Films
include The Lowdown; Exhaust;
Honest; I Just Want to Kiss
You and Hood Felt Hate.
Radio: The Judas Kiss

Toby Whithouse
Writer
Toby trained at the Guildhall
School of Music and Drama
and has been a professional
actor for ten years. Jump Mr
Malinoff, Jump is his first play
and won the 1998 Verity
Bargate Award. He is
currently writer in residence
at the Bush Theatre.

Jonathan Lloyd
Director
Currently Associate Director
at Soho Theatre Company
where he has directed The
Backroom, Belle Fontaine and
Skeleton and run writers'
workshops and an under-11s
playwriting scheme. Other
productions include The
Backroom (Bush); Perpetua
(Birmingham Rep); Summer
Begins (RNT Studio /
Donmar); Channel Four Sitcom
Festival (Riverside Studios);
Serving It Up (Bush); Blood
Knot (Gate) and Function
of the Orgasm (Finborough).
As a writer for children's
television: Dog and Duck
(ITV).

Luke Hunt
Designer
Trained at the University of
Central England, Birmingham,
where he won the Sir Barry
Jackson Award. Theatre
includes Touched by Stephen
Lowe at the Library Theatre,
Birmingham (co-designer).
Prize winner of the 1999
Linbury Award for Stage
Design for this production.

Jason Taylor
Lighting Designer
Productions for Soho Theatre
Company include Kinder-
transport, Tulip Futures,
Site Specific and 5
Plays:4 Weeks. Other designs
include eight seasons at the
Open Air Theatre, Regent's
Park; Rosencrantz and
Guildenstern are Dead
(Piccadilly); And Then There
Were None (Duke of York's);
thirty productions at
Nottingham Playhouse and
The Emaginator, Trocadero.

Matt Mackenzie
Sound Designer
Matt, a New Zealander, joined
Autograph in 1984 and has
designed the sound of several
West End shows for them.
He was Sound Supervisor
for Sir Peter Hall's recent
seasons at the Old Vic and
Piccadilly Theatres, and his
design for Amadeus can
currently be heard on
Broadway.

The Linbury Prize for Stage Design

Luke Hunt was a Prizewinner in the 1999
Linbury Prize for Stage Design for this production
which is sponsored by the Linbury Trust.

The Linbury Prize for Stage Design offers an
outstanding opportunity for talented new
stage designers to work with leading
performance companies at the beginning
of their careers. The biennial Linbury Prize
is worth over £47,000 in prize money, design
commissions and production sponsorships.

Following a showcase exhibition at the
Royal National Theatre in 1999, four designers
were awarded professional commissions with
English Touring Opera, Rambert Dance Company,
Royal Lyceum Theatre Company, Edinburgh
and Soho Theatre Company.

*The Linbury Prize for Stage Design is sponsored by
The Linbury Trust, one of the Sainsbury Family
Charitable Trusts which undertake a range
of charitable activities.*

Sponsored by **The Linbury Trust**

soho
theatre + writers' centre

Soho Theatre + Writers' Centre is the new, permanent home
of Soho Theatre Company who began nurturing new plays
and new writers nearly 30 years ago.

The building includes a comfortable, air-conditioned theatre,
a studio and rehearsal room and also, uniquely, space for
writers – individual rooms to work in and facilities for
seminars and workshops – alongside, on the ground floor,
the award-winning bar and restaurant Café Lazeez.

Hiring the Theatre

Soho Theatre and Writers' Centre has a range of rooms
which are available for hire. Please call Nicole Charalambous
on 020 7287 5060 for further details.

Bars and Restaurant

Gordon's

The main theatre bar is located in the *Café Lazeez Brasserie*
on the Ground Floor. *The Gordon's Terrace* on the second
floor serves Gordon's and Tonic and a range of soft drinks.
Reservations for the Café Lazeez restaurant can be made
on 020 7434 9393.

Free Mailing List

Join our mailing list by contacting the Box Office on
020 7478 0100 or email us at mail@sohotheatre.com
for regular online information.

Soho Theatre New Voices

Our New Voices Annual Membership provides a vital source
of support for Soho Theatre Company's extensive
programme of work. For further details please contact the
development department on 020 7287 5060 or email:
development@sohotheatre.com

Toby Whithouse
Jump Mr Malinoff, Jump

ff

faber and faber

First published in 2000
by Faber and Faber Limited
3 Queen Square, London WC1N 3AU

Typeset by Country Setting, Kingsdown, Kent CT14 8ES
Printed in England by Intype London Ltd

A CIP record for this book
is available from the British Library

ISBN 0-571-20584-4

2 4 6 8 10 9 7 5 3 1

For Helen and Lucas

Acknowledgements

with thanks to
Mum, Dad, Jon,
Mark Ravenhill, Cathy King,
Jonathan, Abigail, Paul
and all at Soho

Characters

Georgei Malinoff (George), sixteen
Nikolai Malinoff (Nick), twenty-three
Pasha Malinoff, fifty-five
Emily Deacon, fifteen
Dougie Price, twenty-three

Non-speaking or offstage characters
Mum
The Only Balalaika Player in Essex

The play takes place in Southend-on-Sea, early 1990s

Notes

The dialogue in < > brackets is in Russian

Osteomyelitis is a chronic infection of the bone.
If after an injury, particularly a compound fracture
such as a bone being broken by a hammer, the wound
is not treated properly there is a danger of the bone
becoming infected and developing osteomyelitis.
The infection forms a sinus which needs regular
daily probing for infection, disinfecting and dressing

Act One

SCENE ONE

Thursday afternoon.
  The café. A counter, cash till, formica tables, tea urn.
Behind the counter is a door leading upstairs, to the rest
of the house, and a serving hatch from the kitchen.
Pinned on the wall next to the door is a picture of the
Queen, and a picture of a square in St Petersburg. The
café is decorated as if for a party. There are streamers
and balloons, and one of the tables is piled high with
food. There is black bread, kvorsh and other Russian
dishes, as well as bowls of crisps and nuts and a couple
of plates of curly sandwiches with little Russian flags
sticking out of them. Hanging over the door right
that leads out into the street is a hand painted banner,
< Happy Birthday Sophia > in Russian, with the letters
getting more and more cramped as it reads to the right.
The sign on the shop door is set to 'Closed'. George
stands by the window, looking left and right up the
street. At the table where he was sitting is a book.
George is wearing a loud Hawaiian-style shirt. Nick is
sitting at the table reading a classic car magazine. He is
wearing a short-sleeved shirt and tie. Sounds from off
the sea, gulls and a little traffic. After a moment Nick,
bored, looks at George, at the food and around the
empty shop.

Nick Hope you're hungry.

George They'll be here.

Nick It's getting on.

George They promised. (*Turns to Nick, concerned.*)

Maybe the trains are delayed.

Nick Nah, they'd have rung.

George Maybe there's been a storm and the lines are down.

Nick Yeah, George, that happens a lot round here.

Pause.

George I've got the only Balalaika player in Essex coming at six. What am I going to say? I spent weeks finding him. He thought I was taking the piss. Said no one's called him since Yuri Gagarin day in nineteen eighty-two. (*looking out of the window*) Mum will be so disappointed . . . (*He glances toward the door leading to the house then sits back at the table.*) I think you're right. What you said earlier, I think you're right. I thought she was getting better . . . When I got back from school she seemed fine, putting the food out, chatting to Lord Mendoza the psychic.

Nick Psychic my arse.

George But when I took her up some tea, the bottle had moved and she was asleep on the sofa.

Nick She'll be alright.

George (*stands*) Do you think I should –

Nick George (*quietly, compassionate*) She'll be alright.

George Yeah?

Nick Yeah.

George nods.

Good man. Make us a cup of tea. As you're up.

George (*sits*) Sod off.

8

Nick laughs.

Nick What you reading, spastic?

George I'm not a spastic.

Nick (*picking up the book*) You are. I've seen you play football.

George Give us it.

Nick (*imitating him*) 'Give us it.'

George Nick . . .

Nick (*reads*) 'On every descendant of the ancient line of Labdacus, divine and bloody retribution shall fall. In the unremembered past some angry God swore vengeance on the whole race, so that anguish and disgrace shall destroy both son and daughter. Another generation sheds its blood, another young root is bared for the same blood-soaked axe – ' Fuck me George, no wonder you don't get invited out much.

George (*grabbing the book back*) It's interesting . . .

Nick Yeah, it'll come in dead handy when you're doing fry-ups here. (*suddenly remembering*) Simon Austin had a fight with Lee Farrell last night in the car park outside the Falcon! I meant to tell you.

George Yeah?

Nick It was wicked. We all gathered round and Paul Gore stamped on Lee's head. I was pissing myself!

George What was it about?

Nick Christ knows. Whatever it was you don't want to make a song and dance about it, Simon Austin's really hard. (*very impressed*) His girl-friend, she's an actress. Did that advert.

George What advert?

Nick Thomas Cook.

George (*equally impressed*) Blimey.

Pause. George looks towards the door.

Nick Joanne Mundy fancies me.

George Yeah?

Nick The word is.

George She's pretty.

Nick She's got a moustache!

George She hasn't, she's nice.

Nick Yeah, if you like girls who look like Magnum.

Voice Off (*slurred, agonised*) Nikolai!

Nick and George stare at each other.

Nikolai!

Nick She's calling you.

George She's calling *you*.

Nick Yeah, but I'm looking after the guests.

George There's no one here.

Nick Might all turn up at once. Never know.

George I could manage.

Nick Out of my hands mate, Mum left me in charge.

George But –

Voice Off Nikolai!

Nick You know what you're like. You'll get in a flap and pour tea on the buns. I'm only thinking of you.

Beaten, George gets up, crosses behind the counter, stands in the doorway and shouts up the stairs.

George < What's wrong Mum? >

Voice Off < Is that you Nikolai? >

George < No, it's George. What's wrong? >

Voice Off < Where's Nikolai? >

George < He's here. >

Voice Off < I haven't had my pills. >

George < You have. I gave them to you when I brought you up your tea. >

Voice Off < Are the guests here? >

George < No, I said I'd call you. They'll be here any minute. >

George comes back into the shop

George Pills.

Nick She's had her pills.

George She sounds tired.

Nick stands, restless, and ambles over to the window.

Nick (*looking out.*) . . . This place . . . (*turning*) Remember that car?

George Car?

Nick The one in Ilford.

George Um.

Nick We'd all gone to see Lydia, and we passed that showroom, and me and you, we looked at that Porsche.

George Oh yeah.

Nick Nine eleven Carrera Coupe. Midnight blue, black interior. Turbo front bumper, G-force suspension, turbo wheels, CD player. Fuck, that was something else. That was like music, that was like stars, that was like sex with . . . I don't know . . .

George Jet.

Nick 'Jet'?

George (*losing courage*) . . . From Gladiators.

Nick Twat! Marilyn Monroe! Lauren Bacall! (*snorts*) *Jet* . . . That'll be me one day, up to London, roof down, shades on.

George Drive down the seafront.

Nick With all the salesmen from Curry's? Fuck that, I'm out of here. Won't see me for dust. Come back one day and piss on the lot.

George It was very expensive.

Nick (*takes out a cigarette*) Yeah well, don't you worry, mate, I been saving.

George You got money?

Nick 'Course. Not telling *you* where. Don't want you nicking it all for Mars bars and Kleenex.

Nick smokes, George watches him, horrified.

George What are you doing?

Nick I'm limbo-dancing, George.

George What if Mum comes down?

Nick What, to 'mingle'?

George They'll be here any minute . . . *Nick* . . .!

Nick smacks his lips, parched.

Sod off.

Nick laughs. Pause.

Don't tell Mum. About the car.

Nick Why not?

George She might get a bit . . . (*Shrugs.*) I don't know.

Nick Has she been saying things?

George No.

Nick What's she been saying?

George Nothing.

Nick George.

George Honest. I'm just saying, you know. That's all.

Nick Eight years . . . For fuck's sake, what does she think I *do* all day?

George I know, it's fine. Don't worry.

Nick sulks and smokes. George looks at the door to the street.

George Do you reckon I will? . . . End up doing fry-ups here?

Nick (*sighs*) I don't know, George, you're smart enough, you'll be alright.

George I got two questions right on University Challenge.

Nick I got them all right on Telly Addicts.

George Mr Bishop says the best qualification is determination.

Nick Bishop is a twat. Always was.

George He's good. He's a good teacher.

Nick You love him.

George Sod off.

Nick You do! I've heard about you in class, always first with your hand in the air, 'Me sir! Me sir! I know the answer!'

George Who told you that?

Nick Dennis Hedges. Well, his dad. He drinks in the Falcon.

George Dennis Hedges stinks.

Nick Listen to it!

George He was caught kissing Gary Forge on the cross country run.

Nick Bollocks.

George He was. And his mum still dresses him.

Nick looks at George's shirt.

Nick Maybe we should get her round.

George What?

Nick Your shirt.

George It's new, do you like it?

Nick It looks like you've been sick.

George Don't you like it?

Nick What do you think?

George Oh. Maybe I should change. Do you think I should change?

Nick What did you put it on for anyway? No one's coming.

Emily, still in school uniform, enters from the street. George leaps up.

George Hallo!

George tries to hide his glee. Nick picks up his magazine.

Emily Alright. Hallo Nick.

Nick grunts.

Charming.

George You came!

Emily Looks like it. Make us a cup of tea.

George OK.

Nick That'll be seventy pence.

George S'alright, I'll get it.

Nick (*smiling to George*) Oh, if you're making one . . .

Emily (*sitting*) Thank you. (*to Nick*) Why can't you be more like your brother?

Nick Just lucky, I guess.

Emily (*noticing the banner and food*) Is all this for your Mum?

George (*flustered*) Yeah, it's her birthday. We're having a bit of a party. We've got some friends coming. Of theirs. From back home. Who live over here now. One's coming from Rhyl! I've even managed to find the only Balalaika player in Essex.

Emily stares blankly back at George.

. . . You've had your hair done.

Nick It looks much better there.

George Nick . . . It's dead nice.

Emily Ta.

George You look like a film star.

Emily My dad says I've got hair like *Howards End*. Did you hear about Sumira?

Nick Who's Sumira?

Emily She's in our class for French.

George Yeah. Twins. Smashing.

Emily Eight pound six and eight pound seven! Imagine that! Makes your eyes water. Says next time she's not gonna stop smoking.

George brings over the teas. Emily notices his shirt.

What's this? New uniform for the staff?

George It's my shirt, do you like it?

Emily Looks like you've thrown up.

Nick *See?*

Emily Why are you wearing it? Is it your national dress?

Nick In case his English teacher turns up.

Emily Well, you look better out of school uniform.

Nick (*indicating his work shirt*) I thought girls liked smartly dressed men.

Emily Show me one and I'll tell you.

George laughs rather over-enthusiastically. Nick and Emily look at him.

So you two looking after the party?

George Yeah, just till Dad gets back. He's gone to get a paper.

Nick puts down his magazine, seemingly shocked and appalled at what George has just said, then bursts out laughing.

Nick *George.*

George . . . What?

Nick I can't *believe* you just said that!

George What?

Nick (*still laughing, to Emily*) He went to get this paper in 1988.

George Nick –

Emily You're joking!

Nick He hasn't been seen since! (*to George*) There's a newsagent at the top of Sinclair Road, what the fuck do you think's taking him so long?

George (*to Emily*) He has been in touch, he sent me a book token.

Nick Oh, this is *priceless*!

George Look, I'm sure Emily doesn't want to hear / about –

Emily Maybe he got lost!

Nick Yeah, it was an *English* paper he wanted?

George We'll talk about it later –

Nick *Mum* doesn't think he's coming back, Pasha *obviously* doesn't think he's coming back –

George You can't say for sure.

Nick No, you're right, it's probably all those supplements, they're a bugger to carry.

Pasha enters from the street. He is wearing an old scruffy suit, his hands are bandaged. Nick stops laughing and goes back to his magazine.

George Alright Pasha.

Pasha (*looks around*) Where is everyone?

George They'll be here any minute.

Pasha It's getting late.

George I think I heard the trains were delayed.

Pasha (*sighs*) Is your mother in?

George She's upstairs, she might be asleep, but go on up.

Nick (*a wicked glint*) I'm sure she'd like to see you.

Pasha looks witheringly at Nick. Then to Emily and back to George.

Pasha < Are you OK? >

George (*lying*) < Yeah.>

Pasha exits through the door into the house.

Emily Is your mum sick?

Nick Yeah, the Judy Finnegan flu.

George Nick . . . (*to Emily*) She's just tired.

Emily Who was that?

George My uncle. Our uncle. Pasha.

Emily He smells funny.

George He doesn't, he's old, that's all.

Emily Hope I die before I get like that.

George Don't say things like that.

Nick Right, I'm going. Can't stand the pace.

George Where?

Nick See Paul. Is that alright, *Dad*?

Emily Can I come?

George Who's gonna look after the guests?

Emily I'll walk with you.

Nick What guests?

Emily Nick –

Nick (*to Emily*) No.

Emily Why not? Free country.

George But Mum left you in charge.

Nick Yeah, and now I'm leaving you in charge, don't have an epi.

George (*sweating*) Fuck's sake, Nick.

Nick And don't swear.

George You can't go, Mum wanted us all to be together.

Nick Yeah, well, not me, you lift her head up when she passes out in the soup. It was bloody difficult getting this afternoon off, I'm fucked if I'm gonna spend it sat here looking at you.

George Do you want another cup of tea, Emily?

Emily I haven't finished this one.

George (*to Nick*) Mum won't like it.

Nick Christ's sake, like she's gonna notice. She's been calling us the wrong names for five years.

Emily Where does Paul work?

Nick Halfords.

Emily That's miles!

Nick (*to George*) Listen to it. (*to Emily*) Stay here then!

Emily My dad says the Gore family are thugs.

Nick (*laughs*) He's right.

Emily Paul thinks he's it. Just 'cos his brother knows Sting.

George Do you want a Coke, Emily?

Emily Shut up, George.

Nick Don't talk to my brother like that.

George I don't mind.

Emily (*to Nick*) You do.

Nick I'm his brother. (*He puts on his coat.*)

George (*brave face*) All the more for us!

Emily (*to Nick*) Nah, you're alright, it's on me way.

Nick (*dryly*) Pinch me . . .

George Have you done that essay yet, for Bishop?

Pasha is standing in the doorway that leads to the house. George doesn't notice him.

Emily No.

George I have.

Emily Do you want a medal?

George I just thought you'd like –

Emily Wait, Nick.

Nick Fuck's sake.

They are almost out of the door.

George (*desperate*) Do you want to copy my homework?

They stop. Nick looks steadily at George for a moment.

What . . .?

Nick Now I know why you put that shirt on . . . Yeah, Emily, come with us to Paul's, we'll have a chat on the way.

Emily (*oblivious*) OK. Later, George.

George Nick . . . < Don't . . . >

Nick (*smiling*) < I don't know what you mean. >

Nick and Emily exit into the street together and disappear. Pause.

Pasha She's watching cartoons. George . . .? You OK?

George Mmmm? Oh, fine. Just a bit . . . (*Shrugs.*) Fine. How are you? Let me see your hands. Ooh, bad yeah?

Pasha The cold doesn't help.

George Shall I change the bandages?

Pasha (*gestures around the café*) But . . .

George 'S'OK, we'll be quick.

Pasha sits down at one of the tables. An almost daily custom, George goes behind the counter, fills a bowl with hot water, takes out a first-aid box and crosses back to Pasha.

Pasha Nick is teasing you again? Have you spoken to him? Like we said? About what they're saying at school?

George He just said I should start getting my leg over a few and prove them wrong.

Pasha sighs heavily.

Pasha Is that black bread?

George Yeah. (*He pops a corner into Pasha's mouth.*)

Pasha (*chews*) Is good!

George begins to unwrap and wash one of Pasha's hands.

George I ordered it from London.

Pasha You are a good boy, George.

George I'll give you a bag to take home, whatever's left.

Pasha (*looking at the mountain of food*) Whatever you can spare . . .

George They'll be here.

Pasha George . . .

George (*end of conversation*) They'll be here.(*He continues to work on Pasha's hands.*)

Pasha Look at those flags!

George They're great, aren't they? I got them from the Labour Club.

Pasha Was Michael there?

George Michael–can't–dance or Michael–new–shoes?

Pasha Michael–can't–dance.

George Yeah, he was there.

Pasha He owes me twenty pounds, did he say anything?

George Not to me . . . Did you finish that Agatha Christie I lent you?

Pasha I did. Very funny . . . The thing is, I am a little temporarily embarrassed . . .

George smiles, gets up and goes to the till.

George How much?

Pasha Ten pounds is all, just until the weekend, until I see Michael.

George opens the till and takes out ten pounds.

Put it in the book.

George It's OK, I'll remember –

Pasha (*adamant*) Put it in the book!

George takes out a petty cash book from the till drawer and makes a note in it.

Who was that with you?

George Emily. Just a mate from school.

George crosses back to Pasha and gives him the ten pounds –

Here you go.

– which Pasha, embarrassed, quickly tucks in his pocket.

Pasha Just until I see Michael . . .

George carries on with Pasha's hands.

She likes you?

George No. Yeah. I don't know, I s'pose so. She's alright.

Pasha I think there is more . . .

George No, we're just – keep your hand still.

Pasha Look at me George.

George Don't –

Pasha I thought so!

George (*trying not to laugh*) It's not like that. Give me your hand, Pasha.

Pasha You can't lie to me!

George Look, she's nice, I like her. (*laughing*) Oh sod off, Pasha!

Pasha I knew it! I knew it!

George Look, don't say anything to Mum. You know what she's like.

Pasha I shall take it to the grave.

George Ta.

Pasha Does she feel the same?

George No. I don't know, I don't think so.

Pasha Why was she here?

George I thought she'd enjoy the party. I got dressed up.

Pasha looks at George's shirt.

George Do you like it? I got it from the market. Fiver.

Pasha (*changing the subject*) My boy is in love!

George You saw her –

Pasha I did.

George – isn't she beautiful?

Pasha She's . . . nice. Her hair, she looks like a poodle.

George (*sighs*) I get so tongue-tied. With you I'm OK, with them I talk such crap. I feel these words come up, and before I can shut my mouth I've said them and they're in the air and the room and I feel so stupid, so . . . young. I told her, oh God listen to this, I told her she looked like a movie star.

Pasha Well, ladies like compliments.

George (*wretched*) Why can't I be good-looking?

Pasha You are good-looking.

George I'm not, Pasha.

Pasha Of course you are. That girl at the Cash and Carry thinks you're good looking.

George She's twenty-eight!

Pasha Even too old for me! Well looks aren't everything, looks fade, you have a spark, personality. Not like Nick with his big talk and . . . hair. You're funny.

George Great, I'll grow up to be the funniest virgin in Essex.

Pasha Ah, is that what this is all about?

George No. (*Pause.*) Yes. Oh, they're all at it, Pasha, they've all lost it except me. Me and Dennis Hedges. I'm never going to do it.

Pasha Rubbish. This is what they tell you.

George It's true! Neville Sugarman and Tracey Gill have been doing it for years! Nick's done it loads of times. With Angela Bailey.

Pasha I've seen her. He is proud of this?

George It's not fair . . .

Pasha I mean, he is *telling* people?

George has finished washing and binding Pasha's hand.

25

George How's that?

Pasha Good!

George (*looks at his watch*) Oh God, look at the time. The only Balalaika player in Essex is coming at six.

Pasha I'm a lovely dancer.

George I gave John the afternoon off and everything . . . It's so embarrassing . . . Give me the other one. (*He starts to unbind and wash Pasha's other hand.*) Actually I'm glad you know. It's such a relief, I've wanted to tell you for ages. It's weird, I'm smiling all the time, I want to run around. Nick's twigged, I think. Funny having a secret. Never had one before. And even though she's gone I can still hear her voice in the room. I think I can smell her shampoo and if I look at where she was standing I can see her. Oh this is horrible, this is hell, this is pain . . . I love it, I love this. I feel alive. I get up in the morning because I know I'll see her at school, I'll pass by her, maybe she'll talk to me. Oh God, it gets too sweet, it burns my brain just thinking about it. I've got her pen, she left it in French.

Pasha Have you told her?

George (*looks at the floor*) No. No, I can't. It would make things difficult. At least like this I can still see her. Nearly finished.

Pasha watches George for a moment, smiling to himself.

Pasha I'm twelve years old –

George Oh God . . .

Pasha – I'm in Saratov –

George I really am fine / about it –

Pasha – and in the next street there's this girl. Irina. Boy, I had it bad for her! I'd wait outside her house for an hour every day to beg her to let me carry her books to school . . . Why I didn't just go there an hour later I've no idea . . . Anyway, this went on for months until finally I say, 'Look, I carry your books for you, when it snows, which is most days, I give you my scarf, I gave you an apple! Would you please let me hold your hand today?' And do you know what she said to me?

George What?

Pasha 'Get away from me, you stink, I feel sick!' (*He smiles triumphantly.*)

George Was that supposed to be helpful?

Pasha (*thinks*) Oh no, wrong story. Sorry.

George Oh bloody hell.

Pasha Ah yes! My other story, I remember!

George I don't know if I want to hear this.

Pasha Maybe this will be useful, maybe not, it can't hurt. I'm, what, eighteen? Full of talk, full of noise like your brother. There was this girl, me and your father, we knew her family. Everyone chatting and laughing all together. But in all that time she and I, we must have said maybe ten words to each other. It was as if from the moment we met there was an agreement between us. There was no need for words. And it was as if everyone else was in on it. 'Have you set date yet?' wink wink. And as time went on I could sense her growing impatient, all around us our friends, her sisters, they were falling in love, getting married and so on. Our moment had come, she was waiting for me to make the move. Part of me was frightened by this, I mean . . . my God . . . but part of me was exhilarated as well, I could feel fate elbowing me in the ribs. But I couldn't do it. Call it cowardice, bravado, stupidity . . . I didn't say a word. Until finally my silence became an insult. Opportunity is a restless guest, he doesn't stay for long. And a year later I'm at her wedding. To your father. And we're sitting around and we're laughing and singing and toasting and my insides are full of needles and stones. And she dances with her new husband, and her father, and then it's my turn. And we dance and we're talking about the priest and I'm saying how lovely she looks and she's saying her friend likes me and I laugh like I'm such a devil, such a *catch*. We just keep on talking, more than we'd ever said to each other in our lives. We pile inanity upon inanity, anything to fill the air between us. And by the end of the evening I'm sick with myself. Sick with this big brave man. (*Pasha takes a tie out of his pocket and puts it on the table.*) I'm thinking maybe Lydia will bring her sister.

George ties it around his own neck to get the knot right, puts it on Pasha, does up the top button on Pasha's shirt, and tightens the tie to his neck.

Age is a penance, to chew on the stupid things you've done. Time yawns, in front and behind, and you worry that life gives you one chance to leap and you just didn't see it at the time. (*He wipes a bead of sweat from his forehead.*) I haven't thought about this in an age . . . It . . . Look at me . . . That's the way with these things. The past is the sea, George. Beautiful, dangerous, waiting. And one day it swallows you up.

George I think I preferred the other story.

Pasha Me too.

Voice Off Nikolai!

George Oh, bloody hell. I'd better go up. Keep an eye out for the guests, help yourself to tea.

*George exits into the house. Pasha sits and looks at
his bandaged hands. Outside, the only Balalaika
player in Essex appears, in full Russian peasant
costume. He peers through the window into the shop,
and taps on the glass.*

Voice Off Nikolai!

Blackout.
  *There is the sound of the sea, the waves lapping
against the shore. The tide coming in.*

SCENE TWO

Saturday afternoon.
  *The end of the day, the café is closed. George is in
jeans and a jumper. Nick is in a new suit, a shocking
electric blue. He smokes while George tidies.*

Nick So we walk in. There's me, Mike, Paul Gore,
Dermot, Mike and Stuart the Greek. Dermot was at
Cubs with one of the bouncers so we got in for nothing.
It's packed out. We have a few beers, but it's getting a bit
boring so we decide to play pull-a-pig.

George Pull-a-pig?

Nick Yeah, what you do is, you look around and find
the ugliest girl in the room and then one of you goes
over, chats her up, dances with her and maybe gets off
with her.

  Pause.

George Yeah . . .

Nick Well, that's it.

George That's it?

Nick Yeah. I mean we buy the bloke a beer, to be fair. So –

George I don't get it.

Nick It's funny, isn't it. Anyway –

George It doesn't make sense.

Nick It doesn't have to make sense! It's a game, not *Murder She Wrote*! Jesus . . . Anyway, we pick Stuart the Greek 'cos he's got olive skin and look around the club for a suitable girl, and who should be on the other side of the dance floor but Debbie Debbie Nixon.

George Debbie Debbie Nixon?

Nick So fat they named her twice.

George Oh, right.

Nick So he goes over and they start chatting, and I've asked the DJ to put on a slow song, and Stuart the Greek and Debbie Debbie Nixon start dancing. I tell ya, we was pissing ourselves. I thought Mike was gonna puke he was laughing so much. Well, they're dancing, and Stuart the Greek is saying stuff like, 'Do you come here often?' and she's like, 'S'pose,' when suddenly she looks over and sees us all laughing. ' 'Ere,' she says, 'are you playing pull-a-pig?' 'Yeah,' says Stuart the Greek, 'we are as it goes. Sorry.' 'S'alright,' she says, 'so are we.'

George No!

Nick Swear to God!

George Brilliant!

Nick I know! It's brilliant isn't it!

George So what did he say?

Nick He's like 'No!'

George I bet.

Nick Still . . .

George What?

Nick The joke's on us really. They're seeing each other again next week.

George Ahhh. That's nice. (*He goes into the kitchen.*)

Nick Fat birds go mad over me.

George (*off*) Yeah?

Nick 'Cos I'm wiry. Their worst nightmare.

> *George re-emerges with two bulging tied-up bin bags.*
> *He crosses to the street door and exits to dump the*
> *bags outside, still visible through the glass.*

George What are you doing here, anyway?

Nick Dropping a Saab off down Burdett Road.

George I thought someone else did that.

Nick Exactly! I think this is a test.

George (*re-entering*) A test?

Nick There's a promotion coming up.

George Ah. Hence the suit.

Nick Hence the suit.

George Where'd you get it?

Nick Gottliebs', up in town. Bloody nice bloke. Shook my hand, called me Sir. 'Would *Sir* like any more room in the leg? Would *Sir* like turn-ups?'

George How much did sir get stung for?

Nick Ninety of your Earth pounds.

George Ninety – ?

Nick It's an investment!

George Did you get a new shammy leather?

Nick Fuck you Rain Man. You could be looking at the new Assistant Forecourt Manager. Mr Healy, *Vincent*, he says candidates must show drive and enthusiasm.

George Shouldn't you be getting back?

Nick (*putting his feet up*) Nah, I'm alright for a bit . . . (*He looks at the floor.*) Was Pasha on today?

George Two till four.

Nick Look at the floor! It's covered in tea!

George More money?

Nick Course. Lots. Well, a bit. Year or so of this, just think where I could be. I can get that Porsche. Then we'll show 'em. Me an' you, up to London.

George Yeah?

Nick Straight up the London Road, don't look back, me an' you, the Malinoffs, the brothers Grimm. Have a drink, have a laugh, get tattooed. Fuck 'em all.

George Fuck 'em all, yeah.

Nick Yeah. Don't swear.

George Nick, Mum asked me if I'd ask you if you'd have dinner with us on Monday.

Nick Can't, sorry, love to, but I've arranged something. (*admiring himself*) I guess I can kiss heaven goodbye, it can't be right looking this good.

George What?

Nick What 'what'?

George What have you arranged?

Nick Business. It's not a game, car retail.

George Sunday then?

Nick We'll see.

George Tuesday?

Nick George give it a rest.

Pasha has entered from the street. He looks at Nick.

Pasha Why isn't he at work?

George He's trying to get promoted.

Nick Have you seen the state of this floor?

Pasha Shocking.

Nick Too right. George is gonna have to clean that up.

George I don't mind.

Pasha I was referring to your suit. What is it you boys have against nice clothes?

Nick That's rich coming from Catweasel.

Pasha (*as he exits into the house*) No wonder she drinks.

George Nick . . . I was thinking . . . do you reckon you could get me a job on the lot?

Nick (*laughing*) Don't be soft.

George No honest, I'd be dead good. I could help out, do the bookwork, that sort of thing. I do most of it for this place.

Nick No.

George Why not? It'd be great, me an' you, the Brothers Grimm.

Nick You've got to stay at school. You've got your exams in a couple of months, they're important.

George Why? What's the point? I'm only gonna end up running this place.

Nick Well, that's not so bad. This could be a nice little earner if . . . (*Shrugs.*) Like Mum says, people will always want to eat.

George But I don't want it.

Nick (*exasperated*) Then don't have it! Flog it, who gives a shit . . .

George Mum wants it to stay in the family, and what with / you at the lot –

Nick George, Mum wants someone to mind the shop while she drinks the fucking profits –

George lunges at Nick, grabbing him by the lapels. They freeze, George just managing to restrain himself from hitting Nick. Pause. He lets go.

George Sorry . . . But you shouldn't talk about her like that.

Nick You see, this is what I mean. You think we owe her something? 'Cos we're family? No way. We're square with Mum, we've been square with her a long time. Jesus H Fuck if you've ripped this I'm gonna twat you I swear.

George But she's our mum.

Nick And we're her sons.

George We have a responsibility.

Nick Yeah and so did she! It cuts both ways! She welshed on us, she welshed on her responsibilities! The other kids, their mums didn't make a habit of throwing up in Asda, their mums remembered birthdays, they didn't have to be cleaned up and put to bed by their children. Fuck *her* George, and that invisible weasel she married. We don't owe them anything. You least of all. (*quieter*) You'd be wasted here. You've got potential, a future. I saw your last report, all those A's. Mum was well impressed, had to put her glass down.

They laugh, George in spite of himself.

You're the smartest one of all of us. Don't be like . . . Don't waste all that on bacon sarnies and cups of tea.

George What about you?

Nick I'll be alright.

George I want to be like you.

Nick (*laughs*) No you don't. You'll be fine. Study, sod the café.

George I hate school, I hate the other kids.

Nick Well, that's what I said when I was your age and I didn't have a big brother to tell me different.

George If you go I'll run away!

Nick What? What are you talking about?

George I don't know, I just . . . I hate it here . . . If you went away it'd be just me and . . . Sorry. (*Shrugs.*) Nothing . . . This promotion . . . (*Shrugs.*) I hate it here.

Nick Don't talk soft. I'm not going anywhere. Not without you, mate. Listen, have you got any money?

George What do you think?

Nick takes out a couple of crumpled notes from his pocket and offers them to George.

What's that?

Nick It's a bunch of flowers George. Go on, the bloke in the shop knocked a bit off for cash. Buy yourself something nice.

George I don't need anything.

Nick Something for Mum then. We never got her anything for her birthday!

George We did. I signed the card from both of us.

Nick Oh. Well. There you are then. (*He makes a big gesture, à la Goodfellas, of giving George the money.*)

George (*looks at it*) This is twenty quid.

Nick Is it? Oh sorry, I need some of that . . .

He takes a tenner back.

Get your exams, then you and me, London, fuck 'em all.

George Yeah . . . *Yeah.*

Pause. Suddenly something outside, in the street, catches George's eye.

Shit. Look.

Nick What?

George Look.

Nick What am I looking at?

George Over there, crossing the road.

Nick (*unimpressed*) Oh yeah . . .

George Do you think she's seen us?

Nick Coming this way.

George (*panics, looks around him*) What shall I be doing?

Nick Eh?

George I want to create a good impression, what shall I be doing?

Nick Um . . .

George I could be preparing food. That would look good.

Nick Tell you what, I'll nip outside, see if I can find a bird with a broken wing.

George Oh shit. Oh shit. Look I've got egg on my jumper.

Nick It doesn't show, calm down.

George Do I look OK?

Nick I'd shag ya.

Emily enters.

Emily Hallo you two.

George Oh! Hallo Emily!

Emily Alright. Alright, Grumpy?

Nick Fine, Dopey.

Emily Not at work?

Nick Keeping an eye on George. Never know who might wander in.

Emily Need looking after do ya, George?

George (*laughs*) Noooo.

Emily Got egg on your jumper. (*to Nick*) Give us a fag.

Nick Like fuck.

Emily Why not? Nearly sixteen.

Nick Not ladylike.

Emily Sod it, I'll have one of my own. (*She opens her bag and takes out twenty Rothmans.*)

George Well done on your French mock.

Emily Oh ta.

George (*to Nick*) She got the highest in the class.

Nick I'll alert the papers.

Emily Second highest, George, you –

George (*quickly*) Highest of the girls.

Emily Oh. Yeah. I s'pose.

Nick looks at his watch and sighs.

Nick Right. Better be going I suppose. Just time to pop something on the six-twenty at Walthamstow. This is it, I can feel it. My palms have been itching all week.

He gets up and speaks quietly to George.

You gonna be alright, monkey boy?

George nods.

Good man. Ta-ra, Emily, *Gladiators* was on earlier, so don't shake his hand.

Nick exits. Pause.

Emily Always in a hurry, that one.

George He's a Leo.

Emily Well, there you are then.

Pause. Emily smokes and looks about her. George is desperately trying to think of something to say.

George I can spit ten yards.

Emily Your parents must be so proud.

George Do you want to see?

Emily Thank you no. Is Nick still going out with Angela Bailey?

George No, she chucked him.

Emily Why?

George Nick reckons she's a lesbian.

Emily Lucky for you my Dad's away. If he caught me in here with a Malinoff, he'd kill you. And skin you.

George Where is he?

Emily Swindon. He goes away a lot on business. Has to stay in hotels, it's horrid he says. He brings me back sachets of stuff, shampoo, body lotion, a shower cap, sewing kit. Dead posh places. I've got the Bristol Hilton, the Stakis Ingrams in Glasgow. He goes all over. Louise Lingwood says the body lotion's made of whale blubber but she's only jealous, her dad drives a cab. Notepaper from the Bournemouth Pavilion, wrote to my cousin with that. Even got a pair of earrings he found in his room in Torquay. Said not to tell Mum, else she'd want some. (*She laughs.*) Men! He loves my hair.

George Did you tell him about your French mock?

Emily He was so proud. 'Brains as well as beauty,' he said. Slapped my back. He would have said more but *Newsnight* was on. Is your Mum feeling better?

George Up and down.

Emily Mmmm. My Mum gets like that. She's taken up the trumpet. Dad says the French never wash.

Emily suddenly notices the floor.

George Oh yeah, sorry about that, it's my uncle, his hands are a bit shakey . . .

George darts behind the counter, gently closes the door to the house, grabs a cloth and starts mopping up the floor.

Emily What's wrong with them?

George Nothing really . . . When he was younger, still back home, he had a bit of an accident. He worked in this factory that made baths and, well, one day his hands got caught in one of the presses. All the bones got broken. It was meant to be turned off, but the bloke at the controls was drunk. His hands weren't treated properly and he got this infection in the bone. Osteomyelitis. The foreman was the uncle of the bloke at the controls, and they wouldn't sign this form that says it was their fault, so Pasha couldn't get a pension or nothing. He says it was mad, *everyone* was crooked. Bandits. The Wild East. He came over with Mum and Dad in 1970. (*indicating the floor*) Some days are better than others. But we couldn't say anything, we couldn't – we're all the family he's got. He never married, you see.

Emily (*hushed, knowing*) Like Mr McIntyre in Sociology?

George No, not like Mr McIntyre. He's just never married.

Emily He should go to the doctors'.

George He doesn't trust them. He doesn't trust anyone really. Doctors . . . Scouts . . .

Emily Do you speak any Russian?

George (*making a joke*) Da.

Emily Eh?

George . . . Yeah.

Emily Go on.

George Vodka.

Emily George – !

George Peter Ustinov.

Emily Stop it!

George It's boring. Mum's English is really crap, so I have to speak it to her all the time.

Emily Pretend I'm your Mum.

George Um, no.

Emily (*pleading*) Just a few words . . .

George (*looks at her and sighs*) OK . . . < Hallo. >

Emily < Hallo. >

George Hallo.

Emily < Hallo. >

George < My name is Emily. > My name is Emily.

Emily < My name is Emily. >

George Very good. < Hallo, my name is Emily. >

Emily < Hallo, my name is Emily. > (*She laughs.*) Nice one! < Hallo, my name is Emily. > Wicked!

George < Hallo. > Excellent. You learn quickly, Skywalker.

Emily Cheers George, more!

George No –

Emily Please!

George OK . . . . Listen to this. < The first time I saw you at school it was like seeing music. I am your dog. Everything reminds me of you. The hand of a baby in a pram, raindrops on a window. It's all you. Your eyes are the colour of Autumn. You are Helen. I want to drink your tears. >

Emily What does that mean?

George (*shrugs and smiles*) Nothing.

Blackout.

SCENE THREE

Wednesday night.
It is raining outside. Dougie Price stands in the middle of the café talking through the serving hatch to Nick, who is in the kitchen making tea. Dougie is wearing a very, very expensive suit. A cashmere coat is hung delicately over the back of one of the chairs.

Dougie – so I'm sat there with Mr Russell. And laid out on the table he's got all my reports and the statements and stuff. And he's looking through them, and he starts shaking his head, so I'm thinking 'Here we go . . . ' And he looks up, and you can see it in his eyes, he's so fucking *pleased* with himself, he's thinking, 'You little shit, just a few more months and you're out of here, you're not my problem any more.' So he sits back in his chair and puts his hands behind his head, like we're old mates, like we're having a *drink*. 'So *Douglas*,' he says, and I'm thinking only my fucking *Nan* calls me Douglas, 'So *Douglas*, where do you see yourself in five years time?' And I'm like, 'I dunno,' and he's like, 'Oh come on, you must have had *some* thoughts on the matter,' and he picks up one of my report sheets. 'The thing is,' he says, 'your little caper with Mr Malinoff, plus your projected results do rather restrict your options.' God, he was such a wanker!

Nick (*through the serving hatch*) Russell? He was alright.

Dougie He was a wanker!

Nick (*thinks*) No, you're right, he was a wanker . . .

Dougie So I'm saying, 'I'll be alright, I'll find something,' and he's thinking, 'Yeah, right, *signing on*,' he's thinking, '*You want fries with that?*'

Nick enters from the kitchen, still in his horrible suit, holding two mugs of tea. He has a joint dangling out of his mouth.

Nick (*the tea*) There you go.

Dougie Smashing.

Nick Three sugars.

Dougie Can't wait.

Nick Just a bag in the mug I'm afraid, it takes ages to get the urn all set up.

Dougie No worries.

Nick (*the joint*) There you go.

Dougie Ta. (*He takes a drag.*)

Nick Paul's got this mate in the T.A. Always gets brilliant stuff.

Dougie (*exhales*) Ding-dong.

Nick laughs. They continue to pass the joint back and forth.

Anyway. 'What you need' he says 'is a *plan*,' and I'm thinking, 'What?' 'For example,' he says, 'at the moment

I'm teaching Maths. Now, ideally in a couple of years I'd like to be Head of Department or maybe a Head of Year. If that goes well, in another five or so I might start looking for a Deputy Head position, if not here then perhaps in another school. And again five years on, maybe more, maybe ten, I'd hope to find myself as a Head Teacher somewhere. That,' he says to me, 'is my plan.' So I say, 'Oh right, I see what you mean. Yeah, I have got a plan as it goes. I'm gonna form a band with a couple of mates and I'll be lead singer. We'll start off just doing pubs and clubs, but at some point we'll get spotted by a producer and he'll get us a three-album contract. We'll start off all hard and subversive and the mums won't like us and we'll have a couple of number ones but it'll be the albums that really sell. Eventually, 'cos I'm the lead singer and the best looking, I'll get taken to Hollywood and I'll make films and I'll win an Oscar. And I'll be so rich I'll buy an island and then I'll get all fat and coked out and I'll have a heart attack on the kharzi. That,' I said to him 'is my plan.' So he says, 'Really Douglas, I think you're being a little unrealistic.' So I says, 'Well you started it.'

Nick You never!

Dougie (*laughing*) Are you sure I never told you this?

Nick So what did he say?

Dougie It all went off. My parents had to come in, he wanted me suspended, you *must* remember.

Nick (*shaking his head*) After the car, Mum and Dad kept me off for a couple of weeks.

Dougie Right . . .

Nick (*still laughing, a bit stoned*) Fuck, that is funny.

Dougie (*reverentially*) Tea!

Nick (*an idea*) Hang about . . .

Nick nips back behind the counter and ducks down, disappearing from view. After a moment he reappears with a half bottle of vodka.

Dougie (*amazed*) She's never still – !

Nick Olympic standard.

Nick gets a couple of polystyrene cups and pours them each a finger or two.

She's got some miniatures in the till as well. If you know where to look it's like Oddbins in here.

Dougie (*toasting*) Nastrovya!

Nick Up your arse . . .

They knock back their vodka, Dougie gets up and looks around the café.

Dougie Look at this place! It's like I never left!

Nick It's a dump.

Dougie It's alright. Nothing a lick of paint wouldn't cure.

Nick Needs knocking down.

Dougie How much do you make here?

Nick No idea really.

Dougie On average.

Nick No idea.

Dougie (*still absently wandering around*) You ever think about getting a place of your own?

Nick Oh yeah, me and Paul are looking for somewhere. It's really difficult, though. Especially if you want something nice and spacious with a bit of garden or something. Everyone's looking to sell, to rent you have to go miles out, like Canvey Island or something.

Dougie (*turns, horrified*) *Canvey*? That's bandit country.

Nick I know.

Dougie Fuck me, even the Kit Kats have got six fingers.

Nick (*laughs*) And it stinks as well. No, we'll find something. Can't wait to get out of this shit-hole.

Dougie looks at the menu board, then turns away and covers his eyes, reciting from memory.

Dougie Chop and chips. Burger and chips. Omelette and chips. Lasagna and . . . don't tell me . . . chips! (*He turns back.*) Well fuck me. That's never the same board . . .

Nick Probably the same chips.

Dougie You ever had venison?

Nick Don't think so.

Dougie There's a little place I know in Finchley, does venison like, what can I say? For the sauce he uses a special combination of lemon juice, orange juice and ground root ginger. I tell ya, it melts in the mouth. We'll go one day, get a booth, take in a club afterwards, make a night of it.

Nick Smashing, yeah.

Dougie sips his tea.

Dougie How's your little brother? He must be, what, fifteen now?

Nick Sixteen, yeah. He's alright. He's a bit of a twat. He's alright.

Dougie I remember him, running around here in his pants.

Nick Hmmm. (*remembering something*) I saw your Tony the other week!

Dougie (*flat*) Is that right.

Nick He'd just got a job, some garage, we had a drink. He said they'd not heard from you for ages. We should all get together.

Dougie (*end of conversation*) We'll see. (*He looks about him, then at Nick.*) Nick Malinoff! (*Dougie shadow punches a few jabs, inches away from Nick's face.*) I couldn't believe it when I walked in the Falcon and saw you sat there.

Nick We're there most nights.

Dougie It's not so much that, I just thought you'd be long gone by now.

Nick Where did you think I'd be?

Dougie Not here.

Pause.

Paul's not changed.

Nick No?

Dougie Nah. Still short, still a twat. (*derision*) Halfords . . . Yeah, that's about his level. Always judge a man by his profession. For example. You remember Matt Piper?

Nick Matt Piper . . . (*the joint*) This is dead.

Dougie Fat kid. Jehovah's Witness.

Nick Um . . .

Dougie He wasn't allowed to come into assembly in case something Christian happened.

Nick (*remembering*) 'I'm not fat, it's glandular!'

Dougie That's him. I bumped into him in London a couple of weeks back. Do you know he's got his own chain of fish and chip shops?

Nick Get away!

Dougie Well, I say chain, it's two really. One in Pitsea, one in Basildon.

Nick Get away! What they called?

Dougie 'Shaddap-A-Yer-Plaice.'

They both crack up laughing, Nick shakes his head in disbelief.

Nick The fat bastard . . .

Dougie No, it was quite nice to see him as it goes. We had a drink. Well, *I* had a drink . . .

Nick He sat on my pipe-rack . . .

Dougie But you see, this is what I'm saying about Paul. Matt Piper may be fat but he's got *drive*. (*contemptuously*) Bikes and car stereos . . . Where's the pride in that? Whereas in my line of work, *insurance*, you're providing a *service*. 'Sure,' you're thinking, 'Insurance! Break-ins and damp and that! Big deal!' But it's the same thing. You live and die by customer satisfaction. And Customers are my Cornerstone.

Nick (*nodding*) Yeah . . . You could say we provide a service an' all.

Dougie Yeah?

Nick The other day I dropped a Saab off down Burdett Road.

Dougie Right . . .

Dougie sips his tea.

Still a sucker for them cars, yeah?

Nick (*beaming*) Paul teases me about it all the time, but he doesn't understand. It's like, even the small crap ones, the Fiats and Renaults, I still get a buzz, you know? I'm in charge of presentational maintenance. Mr Healy likes to deal with all the customers himself. Although he went to an auction once and while Ray was in the toilet I sold a Mini Maestro. About a year ago we had this Porsche. Fuck knows why, no one round here could afford it. But it was like my obsession. I'd get in early every day and polish it until it *glittered*. Mr Healy said if I polished it any more I'd wear the metal away. I'd be looking at it all the time, even when I was having a sandwich or something. It was like we had this *animal* in the yard, like a tiger, all chained up. Eventually a bloke come down from London. He couldn't get over how shiny it was and Mr Healy told him I'd taken a special interest in it. He was really nice actually, we had a chat. And when he went he gave me fifty quid. Fifty quid! I'm like 'Fuck!' So I put it in the Building Society. I've been putting a bit away every week ever since. You see, that's gonna be me one day. The car, the suits, the women. Everything.

Dougie How much you got in there?

Nick Just over two hundred and fifty. I did have more but I took a bit out to get the suit. But there's this promotion coming up and Mr Healy reckons I'm a dead cert. (*He grins.*) Who knows, once I get the Porsche, if I've got anything left, maybe I'll get a suit like yours.

Dougie This is Gibbs of Savile Row Nick. This is fifteen hundred quids' worth.

Nick Blimey.

Dougie Yeah, I know. But it's paid for itself twice over in twat. A Porsche, eh? Well I hope your driving's improved.

Nick Eh? Oh yeah. (*laughing*) The look on your face!

Dougie I was crapping myself! When that copper came along I was *relieved*!

Nick That's nothing. Mr Healy sometimes lets me and Ray test drive new stock. You should see us, we go down Billericay and Wickford on Sunday mornings, it's brilliant!

Dougie (*smiles thinly*) Right . . .

Nick (*grown up*) No, my Mum took it really badly when it happened. She said . . . well, a lot of things. It's funny, I haven't talked about this in years. I've got to be careful who knows, you see. If Mr Healy found out I'd be screwed. Mum went mental. I didn't mean to hurt her, but . . . (*He shrugs.*) I don't know . . .

Dougie These things happen.

Nick Yeah.

Pause.

Yeah.

Dougie My old man went ballistic. He come at me, he was like *Bill Bixby*. Mum was standing between us. 'Don! Your heart!' I never heard the end of it.

Nick You're not in touch any more?

Dougie I'm here five days tops, maybe a week. A friend of a friend is having a bit of money trouble. He owns a restaurant at the top of Pier Hill. I said we'd come and have a look at it, give our professional opinion and that.

Nick No time to see the family then?

Dougie (*shaking his head*) Scrape your shoe and move on.

Pause.

Nick (*grinning at the memory*) The look on your face . . .

Dougie It was like *The Italian Job*!

Nick It was two or three miles at the most before we got stopped.

Dougie Yeah, at ninety mile an hour! (*shaking his head*) You were a mad sod.

Nick Still am.

Dougie (*looks at Nick levelly*) Is that right?

Pasha enters from the house, shaking the rain off. He is wearing an outdoor coat and carrying a video cassette. He freezes when he sees Dougie.

Nick Oh . . . Alright. What are you doing here?

Pasha (*vaguely indicating the cassette, without taking his eyes off Dougie*) Doctor Quinn Medicine Woman. My telly isn't working . . . (*suspiciously, to Dougie*) We've met.

Dougie (*smiles, but doesn't get up*) How're you doing Pasha?

Pasha . . . Dougie Price . . .

Dougie It's been a while. How are those hands?

Nick (*jumping in*) He just strolled into the Falcon and there we were, I couldn't believe it. He lives up in London now, works in insurance, isn't that right Dougie? He's, er, just popped back to help a mate out.

Pasha is looking at Dougie with a mixture of surprise and disgust.

Pasha Car theft to insurance in just eight years?

Dougie (*amiable*) Poacher turned gamekeeper you could say. I was just telling Nick how nice the café was looking. Lick of paint here and there it'd be just like the Savoy Grill.

Pasha (*icy*) Really.

Dougie I'm serious! Nice size kitchen like that, intimate eating area, you could have a right little gold mine.

Nick is trying and failing to stifle his giggles.

Pasha I shall be sure and tell the proprietor.

Dougie You do that. I know a thing or two about restaurants.

Nick (*performing, changing the subject*) I bet you've noticed some changes in town, Dougie.

Dougie (*playing along*) You've got a Body Shop!

Nick Have we?

Dougie I'll tell you something else, I must have seen every different type of baby buggy.

Nick (*shrugs, an explanation*) There's only the one cinema now.

Dougie Well, there you are then . . .

Pasha How long are you here for?

Dougie (*sniggering*) Excuse me?

Pasha How. Long. Are. You. Here. For.

Dougie A. Week. Or. So.

Nick is, by now, barely suppressing hysterics.

I'm playing it by ear.

Pasha Indeed. Well, do let us know when you're going. (*to Nick*) I'll talk to *you* tomorrow.

Dougie (*sweetly*) Ta-ta!

Pasha goes.

Nick Fuck, I'm sorry mate –

Dougie (*laughing*) Ah, don't worry about it.

Nick No, he was bang out of order.

Dougie You can't blame him, suddenly seeing me pitch up after all these years.

Nick Even so, the moody old sod . . .

Dougie Forget it.

Nick He's not my *Dad*.

Dougie Honestly, it's fine . . . So, you seeing anyone?

Nick Ah, you know, bits and pieces.

Dougie Listen to it! They was always chasing after you.

Nick They weren't.

Dougie I'm serious! And there I'd be, fucking Jimmy-no-mates, left with the in-breds. I was always like, 'Alright, I'm Dougie, I'm a mate of Nick's,' and they'd go, 'You know Nick?' and I'd be like, 'Oh for fucks sake . . . '

Nick Long time ago now.

Dougie (*sitting back and straightening the lapel of his very expensive suit*) Innit.

Pause.

Nick Is it true? That story. You and Mr Russell.

Dougie I can't even remember.

He takes a last swig of the vodka.

Coming in today, I, er, passed my old man's shop. I had a bit of time to kill so I went for a wander, old times sake. I can't have been concentrating, 'cos suddenly I looked up and there it was. I mean it's not surprising I missed it, it's a SuperDrug now, but all the same, just seeing it like that, looming up out of nowhere I, er, I got the shakes . . . Twenty seven years my old man worked there, can you believe it? Scraped his way up from nothing he . . . Three kids, never took a day off in his life, he called men our age 'Sir' and swept up their mess and pocketed their change, and nodded and smiled. All his life he never took nothing didn't belong to him. The sort of bloke some Paki in a shop give him twenty pee too much change, he'd go back, ''Scuse me mate . . . ' Oh no, everyone loved my Dad. I bet you all imagined, I bet you all had this little *picture*, the three of us sat at his feet, both bars on, gazing up, 'Daddy!' Well, you're wrong. He was weak. He was a mug. He was a fool. Coming home from school I'd walk a mile out of my way so's I wouldn't have to walk past that fucking barbers' and see that face. And when he retired, his partner and all the customers clubbed together and give him a watch. And the gold plate rubbed off on his wrist. And he nodded and smiled.

Thunder outside, the rain pours.

Listen to that . . .

He goes to the window and peers out into the blackness.

It's funny, the night I left was a night like this. Hot and dry, then rain like something out the Bible. I caught the eight-oh-five from Southend East. We left the rain 'round Basildon. Slight delay at Barking, defective train up ahead. And we sailed into Fenchurch Street about nine-fifteen. I met a man who knew a man. Several men in fact. All had had the same calling. 'Go West my son, and get yourself a job in insurance!' I'll never forget that first night. We found this little place, we had white mussel soup followed by pan-roasted bresse pigeon with chestnuts. Fucked a children's entertainer from Twickenham. Happy days . . .

I'm forgetting myself. That vodka, beautiful.

Nick gets the hint and pours him another cup.

Every man is an island, Nick. You want to write that down. There are no prizes for being a good soldier any more. No one leaps out at the end and shouts, 'Surprise.' Tread on spiders, put your hand in the till, screw your best friend's wife. No one's watching. No one cares. Ever seen a woman so beautiful it staggers you? And you've thought to yourself, 'She's way out of my league'? Not me. Not now. No one lies on their death bed wishing they'd done *less*. And what is it holds us back? Fear. Loyalty. *Sentiment*. When my sister died having her baby, what did I do? Did I moan? Did I give it, 'I'm so sad!' No. I got on with it.

What's Paul up to this weekend? Or Dermot, or Mike? Down some bar, suited up, giving it, 'Look at me I'm a gangster!' Or a family wedding! *(laughing)* Jesus, have you ever – ? Wall-to-wall Moss Bros and a punch up in the car park. Muttering about what a tosser the groom is, 'Yeah, but at least she ain't seeing that darkie any more'. And what then? Some ex-council terrace full of screaming kids, their ears pierced at six months. Half-heartedly fucking the missus and thinking about the girl from the off-licence. Divorced at thirty, with dreams that reach as far as the pub. Or the bookies. Some job. Some *boss*. Propping up the bar staring wide eyed at nothing. Pulling in their stomach as the barmaid walks past. 'Oh yeah, I'm dynamite sweetheart,' their elbow in their own beer. Wearing their attitude and prejudices like a medal, suspicious of books, suspicious of *learning*, proud of their ignorance as if it was fought for. Forty years of boot sales, house clearance, rent, *Exchange and Mart*, hooky perfume, Sunday lunch at nan's, paddling pools, bless the Queen Mum, catalogues, chips, tracksuits, fights, Jobclub, Christmas club, bath night, karaoke night, 'I swear on my babies' eyesight!' Until finally, *gratefully*, they die leaving nothing, not even their son will raise a glass. And I'll bet you this suit there's not one of them don't wake up in the morning, look in the mirror and say to themselves, 'I thought I was gonna set the world on fire.' So how are you gonna get that car?

Enough of this. Why don't you make us another cup of this spectacular tea, I'm just gonna go for a tinkle, and we'll talk some more.(*Dougie gets up.*)

Nick Dougie . . . What *is it* you do . . .?

Dougie I come to the rescue. I'm like those blokes, those – what do you call them? (*He snaps his fingers trying to summon the name.*) Those fucking puppets with the planes . . . Thunderbirds! International Rescue, that's me! It was fate, us meeting like this. (*He puts his hand on Nick's arm.*) Oh Nick, the things you will see.

Blackout.
The sea. Rougher than before, a storm brewing.

Act Two

Thursday afternoon.
  George, in his school uniform, is clearing up some broken cups and saucers from the floor with a dustpan and brush. Pasha stands by, looking sheepish.

Pasha I'm sorry.

George It doesn't matter.

Pasha It wasn't because of my hands, it – the tray was piled too high.

George These things happen.

Pasha Stupid really, I just wanted to get things cleared up before you came back.

George Look, all gone.(*He takes the debris behind the counter. He glances through the serving hatch into the kitchen.*)

Pasha You can take it out of my wages, and that bowl from last week.

George Don't be daft. Where was John?

Pasha I sent him home. (*Gestures around the shop.*) There was no one . . . some workmen . . . He was just stood there over the chip fryer, scratching himself . . . It wasn't because of my hands though. I just put too many cups on the tray.

George Pasha. It's fine.

Pasha Good. Yes. I know. Thank you.

A door bangs, followed by muted voices, off.

Voice Off < Don't go in the shop! We're being burgled! >

Nick (*off*) < What? >

George picks up a pad from beside the till, the orders from that day.

George Is this *it*? For the *day*?

Pasha (*shrugs, an explanation*) It *is* Thursday . . .

George (*sighs*) Right . . .

Voice Off < I heard something crash. >

Nick (*off*) < It was probably – >

George I'm going to the Cash and Carry on Sunday, you want to come?

Pasha Yes / please.

Voice Off < We'll go in together, switch on the lights and surprise them! >

George I'll order the cab for nine-ish.

Nick (*off*) < Switch on – ? It's five o'clock / Mum. >

Pasha Sure.

Nick (*off, sighs*) < Wait there . . . >

Pasha And really, it wasn't my hands . . .

Nick enters from the house.

Nick Mum's up. She heard something crash.

George Yeah, I dropped a tray.

Nick She thought it was night time and we were being burgled.

George I'd better go up. (*to Pasha*) Give me a shout before you go, I'll give you your money for today . . . .

George exits into the house, Nick grabs a Kit Kat or something from behind the counter. Whistling, he starts to make himself a sandwich.

Nick Has she been asleep all afternoon?

Pasha I want to talk to you.

Nick What about? Christ, I'm starving . . .

Pasha What was that boy doing here last night?

Nick Dougie? I told you, we bumped into him at the Falcon. He's just popped back to help a mate out. . . . '*Boy.*'

Pasha What does he want with you?

Nick He was my best mate, I haven't seen him for eight years! We were catching up! (*Nick picks up a piece of broken cup.*) Look at this . . . What's he like?

Pasha . . . He's after something . . .

Nick What are you on about?

Pasha I know that sort. I know *him*! Remember what happened last time he was here? Not all of us have forgotten even if you have.

Nick Oh yeah, like I'd be *allowed* to forget that . . . Have we got any ham?

Pasha So, what was he doing here?

Nick Nothing, he . . . Nothing. (*Nick opens the fridge, takes out an open packet of ham and a jar of mayonnaise.*)

Pasha Nikolai.

Nick Oh give it a rest.

Pasha I tell you that boy is *poison*

Nick He speaks very highly of you.

Pasha I'm just saying, another shock like that could kill your mother.

Nick Well, you'd better not go stirring up any trouble then.

Nick finishes making his sandwich. Pasha watches him.

Pasha Look me in the eye.

Nick What?

Pasha Look me in the eye and tell me you're not up to something.

Nick (*leaning over the counter, leering into Pasha's face and opening his eyes absurdly wide*) I'm not up to something.

Pasha (*after a moment's consideration*) Liar.

Nick How can you tell?

Pasha Your lips are moving.

Nick I don't have to listen to this, I'm having my tea.

Pasha You were always a terrible liar.

Nick You were always a terrible juggler. This is gorgeous . . . (*the sandwich*)

Pasha I knew it! The minute I saw him!

Nick Fuck's sake, *normal* families don't do this! *Normal* people come home, have a sandwich and watch *Newsround*!

Pasha It's just as well your father isn't here . . .

Nick Lucky sod . . .

Pasha Listen to him, always the witty remarks. Never a care for anyone else, never a *thought*.

Nick (*wearily*) Oh Jesus.

Pasha Just don't come running to me for help.

Nick I wouldn't ask for your help if you was the last uncle in Essex . . .

Pasha I tell you that boy is *poison*.

Nick God, you'd love it if I was up to something. Just think, everything you've ever said about me, you'd be right. You'd love that, it'd make your day.

Pasha We *know* you, Nick Malinoff.

Nick looks at Pasha for a moment, chewing on his sandwich.

Nick (*a decision*) Well, you're in for a treat then. (*Nick smiles, puts his sandwich down, pushes the plate aside and lights up a cigarette, relishing every moment.*) Dougie's offered me a job.

Pasha You . . . you have a job.

Nick (*chuckles*) Oh, not like this. This is a one-off, a favour.

Pasha (*fearing the worst*) I take it it's not insurance-related.

Nick *That*, Tovarisch, is where you're wrong.

He speaks slowly, dramatically, savouring the effect it's having on Pasha.

There's this big restaurant in town. The bloke who owns it is in a bit of trouble, gambling or something. He owes all this money to these people. Well, they suggested he get in touch with Dougie. Dougie has this sideline you see. Him and a couple of others, mates of his from London . . . (*He takes a long drag on his cigarette.*) . . . They burn down buildings.

Pasha . . . Oh my God . . .

Nick Dougie's offered me a place on the team, he reckons I've got just the right stuff. That's the *mate* he's come to help out: they've been planning an accident. Something quick and massive and Dougie wants me there. This is it, Pasha, this is my ticket out of here, and I *cannot wait*. 'Cos I'm thinking if I do alright Dougie might offer me a permanent position. Then London, *Bam*! Won't see me for dust! There, you *happy* now? All those years, all those comments, you were *absolutely right*!

Pasha Oh my God. Oh my God. Oh my God.

Nick (*contemptuous*) Yeah, I thought that'd cheer you up.

Pasha How *could* you – how could you *do* this to us?

Nick (*chewing*) It's a scandal, isn't it?

Pasha After all they did, after everything . . .

Nick I blame the parents.

Pasha (*pacing, wailing*) Dear God, not again!

Nick Alright, don't have an epi.

Pasha It's happening all over again!

Nick Keep your voice down, you want Mum to – !

Pasha The *work*, the humiliation – !

Nick Look it's all above board and everything, everyone's consenting –

Pasha For nothing, for *this*!

Nick Jesus calm down. The restaurant will be closed, the blokes I'll be with know what they're doing, it'll be like an accident. I get paid, the staff get paid, the bloke who owns it gets the insurance, everyone's happy.

Pasha So why can't Dougie do it himself?

Nick He's – I can't remember.

Pasha Try.

Nick He's somewhere else. He has to be somewhere else.

Pasha Nick, you must be a very special kind of stupid. Of course he's somewhere else, he doesn't want to take any risks, it's illegal!

Nick . . . Technically.

Pasha *Technically*? And what if you get *caught* technically?

Nick Why would we get caught?

Pasha . . . Someone might report you.

Nick Who?

   Pause. Pasha stares defiantly at Nick.

Don't make me laugh.

Pasha I could.

Nick Go on then. Phone's upstairs, help yourself. And let's see how much your precious George loves his uncle Pasha then. Eh? Your little soldier?

   Pasha doesn't move.

Go on. Friday night, ten thirty, Alfredo's. Give us a pen, I'll write it down. Big restaurant, top of Pier Hill opposite Tny and Guy, you can't miss it. Shame about those lovely pally chats you have of an afternoon, they'd stop. Can't imagine anyone wanting you around that much. Still, I'm sure you'll find something. Fifty-five-year-old Russian immigrant with manky hands, there must be people crying out.

   But you could cope with all of that. Except George.

Sound off, George coming down the stairs.

Mmm *mmm*. I tell ya, one day someone is gonna write a *song* about that sandwich.

George enters from the house.

Georgie!

George crosses to the other side of the café to pick up his school bag, talking as he goes.

George It was really funny, we've got this fat kid in our class called Kenny and he was mucking about and Miss Brecon caught him and made him stand up and recite the verb 'to eat'.

Nick I guess you had to be there..

George Oh, sod off.

George exits into the house. Pasha has stood up and is getting into his coat.

Nick Where are you going?

Pasha Your mind is obviously made up. So there is nothing I can do. Except be here to pick up the pieces of your family afterwards. Again.

With difficulty Pasha starts to button his coat. Nick watches him.

Nick (*sighs, taking pity*) Look . . . you don't – wait a sec, you don't understand, I was always the *Boy*, it was always gonna be me who made it. I had all this promise, all this – I know it sounds stupid, but when they picked teams and that they'd always pick me first. Just waking up in the morning I was so excited. Everything was waiting for *me*, itching for *me*. When did it all change? Look at me, I'm twenty-three. I spend my day sponging down second-hand Vauxhall Cavaliers. What have I got to look forward to?

Pasha Maybe if you'd paid a little more attention at school instead of running around stealing cars like a bandit we wouldn't be having this conversation.

Nick That is your answer for *everything*!

Pasha That it should come to this, my own family . . .

Nick It's six hundred quid, do you know how long it takes me to *earn* that sort of money?

Pasha Our *name* Nick, our *name*!

Nick What are you talking about?

Pasha Your name is our name!

Nick Since when has that been anything to brag about? We've got a crippled uncle, an alcoholic Mum and a disappearing Dad! Fucks sake, we're not exactly the Osmonds!

Pasha How can you talk this way about your *family*? About your *home*? The sacrifices they made for you and George.

Nick You didn't seem too proud of your home on the boat coming over to England.

Pasha Only a child could / say that!

Nick Where was my family eight years ago? Where was my *home* then?

Pasha If you had any idea what they went through to raise you here / you would not ask.

Nick Oh Jesus, here we go, blah blah blah, lots of forms, lots of money.

Pasha (*almost to himself*) Such disrespect. Dear God, if you knew.

Nick Bullshit! Where's the respect in a greasy spoon café on Southend seafront?

Pasha *Such respect is earned*! From a seventeen-hour day that puts food on the table for you and your brother! Respect lies in bread and in sweat, not in fast cars and suits!

Nick Well there's a tempting picture. You want me to turn down this opportunity for that?

Pasha I want you to turn it down for you.

Nick For *me*? So that one day I can have a life like you lot? A shitty home, a shitty job, or pissing my life away at the bookies and the Labour Club? No way, I won't do it Pasha! I'm better than that, *I'm not George*!

Pause. They stare at each other.

Voice Off Nikolai! Nikolai!!

Pause.

Pasha You want to hear a story? Whenever Stalin made a speech the applause went on for hours. You know why? Because nobody would dare to be seen to be the first to stop clapping. After we arrived in this country it took years, *years*, before any of us could sleep comfortably at night, without fear of a step on the stair. Who are you to give me such a lesson? (*He holds up his hands.*) You think I need *reminding*? Your naivety makes me sick. They worked all their lives to put food in your ungrateful mouths and you spit it back saying it's not good enough, it 'depresses' you. They risked their lives to escape from fear and greed and find their house has been set on fire by their *children*? Damn you, Nikolai. Damn your ungrateful bones. You're right, get out. Buy your car and do your grubby business and get out. Don't dirty our name with yours any more.

Pasha leaves just as George enters from the house.

George Where's he gone? He didn't even say goodbye . . . What were you arguing about?

Nick Nothing. Sport.

George Mum was dead worried.

Nick She'll live.

George In Art we had to do a picture of a member of our family. I did you.

Nick Yeah?

George Left it on the bus.

Nick (*pulling on his coat*) Nice one.

Nick exits quickly into the street. George shouts after him.

George Fish fingers tonight!

George watches Nick go. He turns, sighs wearily, and starts to dispose of the broken cups and saucers as the lights fade.
Blackout.

SCENE FIVE

Very late. Dark, except a light from the kitchen which spills out through the serving-hatch, illuminating Nick sitting at one of the tables, Mum's bottle of vodka in front of him. There is a knock on the shop door. Nick gets up, looks out through the window, unlocks and opens the door. It is Emily, almost unrecognisable in a puffa jacket and baseball cap.

Emily Alright.

Nick We're closed love.

Emily It's me, Emily. George's mate. I've got a hat on.

Nick . . . Emily?

Emily We're not mates really. We're in the same group for French. I think he's a bit funny. *Curieux.*

Nick What are you doing here?

Emily Fancied a drink. I saw the light and took a chance.

Nick I told you, we're closed.

Emily Don't be snippy, I've brought me own. We can have a party.

She takes two cans of beer out of her coat pockets and walks past Nick into the café.

Nick It's gone one, your parents know you're out?

Emily Dad's in Stevenage till Tuesday. Don't worry, we're quite safe. Promised me a pen.

Nick What about your Mum?

Emily (*laughs*) My Mum.

Nick You shouldn't be here. If the police come in – we haven't got a licence to consume alcohol.

Emily Like they would. (*indicating the vodka*) Besides it looks like you're having a party as it is.

Nick There are people upstairs. *George* is upstairs.

Emily (*handing Nick a can*) We'd better be quiet then.

Nick Where'd you get these?

Emily The offy.

Nick looks at her sceptically.

Honest. I get stuff from there all the time. Everyone says I look dead old for my age. It's 'cos I'm tall see. (*flirtatiously*) Long legs. Don't you think? They run in the family.

Nick Well they would. Have you been crying?

Emily I like it in here. Dark. Turn that light off, I bet you could get up to all sorts, no one would see a thing.

Nick (*handing her back the can*) Go home, Emily. You're out of your depth.

Emily Maybe I like it like that. Your brother's good at languages.

Nick (*taking her arm and ushering her towards the door*) Yeah, he wants to join the Foreign Office. Come on, it's late, I'm not fucking about.

Emily (*stopping him*) I'm nearly legal. A month off.

Nick Seventeen are you? Besides, it's not just that.

Emily I don't mean drinking.

Pause.

Ten minutes?

She holds out the can, after a moment he takes it.

Nick Five.

Emily quickly tugs off her jacket before he changes his mind. Nick opens the can, the beer fizzes and spurts out.

Emily Yum.

He looks at her.

Must be great living above a café. All that food. I'd be like Debbie Debbie Nixon if I lived here. Bet you get the pick of all the girls and all, the customers. Like flies round muck I bet. 'Cos you're not like blokes round here, you're different. That's the first thing I noticed when I saw you that time. Do you remember it? We was in town, I was standing outside Keddie's with Louise and you walked past with George and George was laughing about something and Louise says, 'Who's that with George?' and I'm like, 'I don't know,' and she's like, 'Call George over,' and I'm like, 'No!' and she does it anyway and she's like, 'George!' and he looks over and comes over and you're still standing where you stopped outside Hennes', and Louise is talking to George about History or something and I'm not listening and just looking over at you and George is like, 'Alright Emily,' and I'm like, 'Alright George,' but I'm still looking at you and you're looking back and you've got a cigarette and you look like James Dean in that film but your hair was longer then and Louise says, 'Who's that?' and George says, 'It's my brother Nick,' and I'm like, 'Nick,' and then George says, 'Seeya,' and we're like, 'Seeya,' and he goes back to you and you walk down towards the sea-front and we're like, 'Phwoar!' and you was wearing a denim jacket and it was October. Do you remember?

Nick No.

Pause.

Emily Oh.

Pause.

Louise is a vegetarian.

Pause.

I think about that time.

Pause.

George told me about Angela Bailey. You're best out of it, she was an ugly cow if you ask me. And the gob on her! (*Sings*.) 'You've got more rabbit than Sainsbury's!' That's her. (*Pause. Sings*) 'Vous avez plus de lapin que Sainsbury's!'

Nick Time's up.

Emily That was never five minutes.

Nick I changed my mind.

Emily I haven't finished my beer.

Nick Look, I'm not in the mood, I've got a lot on at the moment –

Emily Tell me.

Nick Come on –

Emily I'm interested.

Nick Emily –

A shadow breaks the light from the kitchen, Nick and Emily don't notice.

Emily I'm annoying I know. Apparently I'm at that difficult age.

Nick Well twenty-three's a bloody difficult age if you ask me.

Emily There. You understand.

Nick What?

Emily I knew the minute I saw you, you know what it's like.

Nick . . . What do you want, Emily?

Emily (*shrugs*) A nice word. (*Shrugs*.) A tickle.

Nick looks away.

What's stopping you? I can be dead grateful.

Nick If someone came in, it wouldn't look right.

Emily They won't. It can be our secret.

Nick I *live* here.

Emily You telling me you haven't thought about it?

Nick George / . . .

Emily You've been giving off signals.

Nick Emily. Please. Go home.

Pause.

Emily . . . I can't.

Nick Why not?

Emily I'm frightened.

Nick Of what?

Emily It's not 'cos of what you think. There's nothing like that. But I'm so frightened all the same.

Nick What are you frightened of?

Emily I don't know. Me.

Nick (*gently*) Everyone's fucked up at fifteen –

Emily We're not good people, Nick.

Pause.

I'm not making sense. I wish I could say it in Russian.

Nick smiles, she smiles too.

There. Made you smile. Look at you. You're like someone in a song. She must be mad chucking you,

you're lovely. An international playboy, woman in every airport like Bryan Ferry.

They smile, pause.

They never told us it was like this, did they?

Nick . . . No

Pause.

Emily You're right. It's late.

Nick . . . Every man is an island.

Emily Eh?

Nick No one's watching. No one cares.

They kiss.

Emily That was nice. We escaped. Just for a minute.

They kiss.

You taste like aftershave.

Nick Got it in a magazine.

They kiss.

Emily Glad I came?

Pause.

Nick You haven't come yet.

Blackout.

SCENE SIX

Even later that night. Pasha is dozing, his head on his arms, at one of the tables. After a moment George enters quietly through the shop door. He touches Pasha gently on the shoulder. He wakes with a start.

Pasha Who is there? Who is it?

George It's me.

Pasha George . . .

George Hallo, I'm sorry –

Pasha (*furious*) Where have you been? It's three o'clock.

George Is it? I'm sorry . . .

Pasha pads over to the wall and turns the lights on.

Pasha Your mother is worried sick, where have you been?

George I was on the beach.

Pasha The beach? All night?

George No, I was out. Is Nick here?

Pasha No, he's out looking for you. Why didn't you come home?

George I couldn't.

Pasha Stupid boy!

He cuffs George across the back of the head, then hugs him impulsively, then hits him again.

You do this to your mother! To me! You think we don't worry enough? George . . . (*Sighs.*) From Nick we expect such stupidity, but from you . . .? What were you thinking of?

74

George I don't want to talk about it.

Pasha Oh no no no no no, is not so simple. I've been out looking for you as well, I only just got back.

He puts his hand to his chest.

God in heaven you gave me a fright. Look at me, I'm sweating! Gentlemen of advanced years weren't made to sweat. Now, you tell me what this is all about, then we go and tell your mother. Take your time, I want my heart to start beating normally. Do I look pale? I feel pale . . .

George I've been out.

Pasha This we have established.

George Pasha . . . I saw them.

Pasha Who?

George Nick and Emily. Tonight.

Pasha What? Where?

George Here. I came down, I thought I heard voices.

Pasha I don't . . . What were they doing?

Pause.

Oh my boy. Oh my boy, I'm so sorry . . . Are you sure?

George I saw them through the serving hatch. They were sleeping together. On that table.

George and Pasha look at the table.

Pasha Did they see you?

George shakes his head.

I don't know what to say . . . I put the kettle on.

He starts toward the kitchen, but stops before he reaches the door. Slowly he tries to clench and unclench his fists.

That boy. Georgei . . .

George stands facing Pasha. Gradually he begins to cry. Pasha hugs him.

Good boy. That's it. Never again . . . Never again . . .

He takes a step back to look at George.

Better?

George No.

Pasha No, me neither.

George I'd better go and see Mum. Has she been . . .?

Pasha A bit. To calm her nerves.

George (*sighs*) Great . . . Don't leave me up there too long. Would you make some tea?

Pasha Of course.

George moves toward the door.

George . . . Did he know?

George Oh yeah. He knew.

Nick enters from the street, he makes straight for George.

Nick Where the fuck have you been?

Pasha Nick –

Nick You gave us all a heart attack, disappearing like that!

Pasha (*to George*) Go and see / your mother, quickly!

Nick Mum's going mental, she was just about to call the police!

Pasha Nick, *leave* him.

George I –

Nick What are you talking about, I've been out looking for that little sod!

Pasha You don't / understand –

Nick I went all the way up to Southchurch Park, it's freezing out there!

Pasha George, I won't tell you again.

Nick Just as well Dad *is* getting a paper 'cos you'd have got a right / kicking.

Pasha (*almost pushing George out of the door*) Go!

Nick Look at my trainers!

George has gone.

Well? What was that all about?

Pasha Nick –

Nick Has he seen the time, some of us have got to work in the morning.

Pasha *Nick*!

Nick What?

Pasha . . . He saw you. With Emily.

Pause.

Nick I don't know what you mean . . .

Pause.

Fuck.

Pasha (*dryly*) Well, exactly.

Nick How?

Pasha He lives here! (*derision*) 'How' . . .

Nick Fuck . . . Is he OK?

Pasha He'll live. We all 'live'.

Nick I've got to talk to him . . .

Pasha scrutinizes Nick.

Pasha You knew. You knew. How he felt. What she meant. And still you do such a thing. You treat your brother like a stranger.

Nick You don't understand –

Pasha I understand better than you think perhaps.

Nick Look, I don't know what he said he saw –

Pasha It was hardly a matter of interpretation! People like you . . . You are bad news for this family Nick, you are bad news for George. I can't let you hurt your brother like this.

Nick (*snorts contemptuously*) You're the last one to talk.

Pasha What?

Nick All this bullshit, 'the family, the family,' everyone's best mate. Let's face it, it's not the cups of tea keeps you hanging 'round here.

Pasha slaps Nick across the face.

Ow.

Pasha Ow. I try to tell you something about *decency*, about being a *man*, and you talk about your *mother*? You compare what you did, to how I *feel*? Is that what you think I've been doing all these years? Even with my brother gone, I could *never* . . . You reduce everything to your own grubby simplistic level. (*Pasha stares at Nick as if seeing him for the first time.*) Who are you . . .? What have you become . . .?

George enters from the house. Silence.

Nick George . . . I'm sorry mate.

George Sorry's for breaking my bike, Nick.

Nick I can explain.

George Really?

Nick glances at Pasha.

Nick Not here. Give us a knock before you go to bed. Or in the morning, we'll talk then, yeah?

George doesn't respond.

I . . . I don't know what to say.

Pasha Try 'Goodnight'.

Nick Mate . . .?

Still George doesn't respond. Eventually Nick shambles off. Pause.

George It's not fair. She doesn't *mean* anything to him.

Pasha moves over and stands next to him. Their hearts in pieces.

Pasha No, George . . . This must stop.

Long pause. Pasha looks at his hands.

I need to tell you something. It's about Nick. It's about something he's going to do.

George What . . .?

Pasha (*slowly, deliberately*) Some people . . . are just bad. They just *take* and they don't care who they step on, who they hurt. They are not like us. Like men. All your life they will find you. All your life they will Seek. You. Out.

79

This . . . what I am going to tell you . . . this is my *gift* to you. What you do with it is up to you. But it has to be your decision. It has to be you who makes the call.

This . . . my gift . . . I am giving you your freedom.

Blackout.
There is the sound of waves crashing against a shore. Gradually it builds in volume and violence until it sounds as though they are crashing against the very walls of the café.

SCENE SEVEN

Friday afternoon.
Nick is sat in a chair by one of the tables. He has a large tea towel tied around his neck like a giant napkin. Dougie stands in front hopping excitedly from foot to foot. He has two plastic spoons in his hand. There are two Tupperware tubs on the table. The sign on the door is set to 'Closed'. Dougie carefully takes a spoonful of the contents from one of the tubs and gently feeds it to Nick, who rolls it around his mouth for a moment.

Nick It –

Dougie (*silencing him*) Ah! (*pointing at the tub*) 'A'.

Using the clean spoon, Dougie carefully takes a spoonful of the contents from the other tub, which he again gently feeds to Nick. Dougie points at the second tub.

'B'. There. Now, as I said, one of these is off the shelf from Marks and Sparks. The other I made myself. OK. First impressions.

Nick Both really nice.

Dougie 'Both really nice.'

Nick Yeah, fresh. Tangy.

Dougie 'Tangy'? Hmmm. OK, texture. Which had the best texture?

Nick A.

Dougie A.

Nick A was more textured.

Dougie Right . . . Flavour.

Nick Flavour? Well . . .

Dougie Do you want to try one of them again?

Nick No I'm alright . . . Um . . . B.

Dougie B? How would you describe B's flavour?

Nick That's tricky.

Dougie I mean, would you say it was savoury? Or sharp? Or minty like a mint? Or spicy?

Nick Savoury, I think.

Dougie 'Savoury.'

Nick But you see A was more creamy.

Dougie Was it?

Dougie takes a pen and notebook out of his pocket.

Nick Yeah, and that was really nice as well.

Dougie (*scribbling furiously*) This is all *very* helpful.

Nick Dougie . . .

Dougie Yes, sweetheart. (*He looks up, a gleeful smile.*) Isn't this fun? Don't get me wrong, I love my job, but if I had my time again I'd be a chef. The blokes at the top, we're talking silly money.

Nick Tonight . . . No one gets hurt do they?

Dougie Oh yeah. You'll be picked up about ten. You're just gonna be on look-out tonight, holding the coats so to speak, we're going to ease you in gently, it's a lot to take in in one go. But take my advice and keep your eye on Trevor. Don't ask me how he does it but the man's a natural. In fact I'm gonna try and set you up a workshop with him next week. No, it's a gift what he's got. Like golf. Or the piano. There shouldn't be any trouble, Alfredo's is closed for 'refurbishment'. I've booked us all a room at the Falcon for afterwards, we'll have a drink. 'Savoury' . . . Well well well.

Nick The thing is . . . I've been having a think.

Dougie . . . Oh yeah?

Nick Don't get me wrong, I'm really tempted and that, but things have got a bit complicated and –

Dougie . . . What's that?

Nick . . . I think I'm gonna have to say no . . .

Dougie (*looks up*) 'No'?

Nick Yeah.

Pause.

Sorry mate.

Pause.

Dougie I'm afraid it's not so simple. This isn't like going for a swim on the beach and you can just pop in and out as the mood takes you. You can't just dip your toe.

Nick . . . What do you mean?

Dougie I've made phone calls. You've got the Dougie Price seal of approval, that counts for something.

Nick Yeah, but –

Dougie You want to spend the rest of your life in Southend? Getting pissed and working on the lot? Is that gonna get you your Porsche? Fuck me, 'time you can afford that we'll all be living on the moon.

Nick Even so –

Dougie What happened with that promotion?

Nick . . . Mr Healy's got a nephew . . .

Dougie (*smiles sympathetically*) Like I said, I come to the rescue. I'm like Red Adair. . . . Actually that's quite ironic when you think about it . . .

Nick I don't want rescuing.

Dougie You say that now. It's first night jitters. (*He winks conspiratorially.*) I quite understand, I was the same myself. Trust me, we'll laugh about this tomorrow.

Nick It's my family you see, they . . . I think it's best. I'm dead grateful and everything but, really, it's just not for me.

Dougie (*back to his tubs*) Not for you. How quaint. Now just a few more questions.

Nick Dougie –

Dougie In terms of a favourite . . . A or B?

Nick (*sighs*) I couldn't say. Look, Dougie –

Dougie No, come on, I won't be offended.

Nick They were both really nice.

Dougie Even so, you must have had a favourite.

Nick No, really –

Dougie There must have been one you liked a *bit* more.

Nick There was nothing between them honest. I just want to sort this out –

Dougie Come on, A or B. I won't mind, I promise.

Nick I can't say.

Dougie I've got a gun to your head. Pretend. I've got a gun to your head and if you don't make a decision I'm gonna blow your brains out all over the tea urn.

Nick Oh for fuck's sake –

Dougie It can't be *that* hard.

Nick . . . I don't know. (*Shrugs.*) A.

   Pause.

Dougie (*flat*) A.

Nick (*pointing*) That one.

Dougie Yeah, I know which one A is.

Nick A. A was terrific.

   Pause.

Dougie What's wrong with B?

Nick Oh Jesus.

Dougie No no, it's fine, I asked for your opinion.

Nick Look B was –

Dougie A it is.

Nick (*exasperated*) I meant B. Definitely B. B is the best. The best soup I've ever had in my life.

Dougie No, you said A was best. Mass-produced-brewed-in-vats-in-Bradford-A. While B, hand-made-with-skill-and-love is shite. Is sick. Is the jizz of a syphilitic leper.

Nick Dougie –

Dougie Have you ever tried to find Marjoram in Southend?

Nick They were both dead nice.

Dougie Well, one of them obviously wasn't.

Nick Maybe if it was hot . . .?

Dougie 'Hot'? IT'S GAZPACHO! It's a summer soup! It's not meant to be hot!

Nick Dougie *listen* to me! *Tonight. I'm out. I'm not doing it. It's what I've decided.*

Dougie grabs Nick by the throat, pushing him back until he is bent backwards over the table, spilling the Gazpacho everywhere.

Dougie You've *what*? It's what you've *what*? It's what you've *decided*? Well well well, how interesting. Cunt's got an opinion all of a sudden.

With his free hand, in one fluid movement, Dougie pulls a barber's shaving razor out of his pocket and holds perilously close to Nick's face.

I don't care if you've *decided* to stick a Fiat Punto up your arse!! You're my puppy, you don't change channels without my say so!! IS THAT CLEAR? CAN YOU HEAR ME HOUSTON? *THIS* IS ME! *THIS* IS ME!! I'M DOUGIE PRICE!!

They stare at each other. After a moment Dougie lets go of Nick's throat, but Nick stays sprawled over the table, frozen with surprise and terror, his elbows in the pools of soup. Dougie folds the blade up and swiftly pockets it again. He calms himself down, taking a couple of deep breaths.

I hope that clears things up. Look at you. So full of shit your eyes are brown. You thought you could wander in and out of my world like a tourist. (*He shakes his head.*) You're Lost in Music, sunshine.

I disgust you don't I? You wanted to walk with giants, be the big 'I am' and all you got was me. I'm the unacceptable face of everything you want. I'm the price.

Dougie picks up a napkin and starts dabbing off spots of soup from his suit.

See this is just the beginning. I've got plans for you, Nick Malinoff. You're gonna be My Man in Havana . . . Well, you know what I mean . . . If ever I call you, you'll be there. If ever I tell you to jump you'll ask 'How high?'

He tosses the napkin back at Nick. Pause.

How's your little brother? He must be what, sixteen now? God there's an age, do you remember it? All elbows and spots. Yeah, how is he? How's *George*?

You'll do this job for me. Oh, I think you will.

You're nothing Nick. You're white trash and you're nothing.

'Maybe if it was hot.' Jesus, you can tell we're in Essex . . .

Blackout.

SCENE EIGHT

Friday night.
    The café. Dark. Nick stands facing Emily.

Nick It's late.

Emily I've been waiting for you.

Nick So I see.

Emily You alright? I went to the lot, they said you hadn't been in since lunch.

Nick No.

Emily I wondered if you fancied a drink.

Nick Isn't it a school night?

Emily Friday.

Nick (*mutters*) 'Course. Um . . . not tonight, I've got something on.

Emily Tomorrow night?

Nick No.

Emily That only leaves Sunday and everything's shut then.

Nick No, Emily.

Emily Well when?

Nick What part of 'No, Emily' don't you understand?

Emily I'm only saying . . . What's that on your top?

Nick Um, Gazpacho. It's a summer soup.

Emily (*smiles, doting*) What are you like?

Nick Have you seen George today?

Emily No, I wasn't at school.

Nick Oh.

Emily Too excited.

   Pause.

I love you.

   Nick looks at her.

Nick Fan*tastic.*

Emily (*sighs with relief*) There, I've said it.

Nick Jesus.

Emily Look at my hands, they're shaking!

Nick You don't, Emily.

Emily And I've been practising.

Nick I really need this . . .

Emily Last night was wonderful. I'm floating. Cloud nine.

Nick It shouldn't have happened.

Emily I knew from day one.

Nick What?

Emily I rang Louise, she's dead pleased for us. There's a funfair in Chalkwell next week, we can go.

Nick What happened last / night, it –

Emily Mum can't wait to meet you.

Nick Look you're a smashing girl and everything but, I mean, you and me? Come on –

Emily What?

Nick Look, I'm not saying it wasn't a laugh but I've got a lot on my plate right now –

Emily I don't understand.

Nick I'm just saying it wouldn't –

Emily What –

Nick Come on, Emily, be reasonable, can you imagine you and me? Meeting my mates, my Mum and Dad? / It's –

Emily Of course –

Nick Can you see us going on a date?

Emily We could go bowling.

Nick Are you listening to me?

Emily Nick –

Nick No us, Emily, no golf with your Dad, no 'You put the phone down first'.

Emily I don't care about my Dad.

Nick I'm telling you once. You stay away from me, away from my family, and most of all stay away from George.

Emily Or what?

Nick I'll bury you.

Thunder rumbles, low, in the distance.

Emily So that's it? You leave me with that? You're bad Nick Malinoff.

Nick Bad as I was last night?

Emily Don't be like this.

Nick . . . It's me.

Emily But we escaped.

Nick Yeah. But they caught us in the end. They always catch you in the end.

Emily Yeah.

Emily slowly makes her way to the door.

I won't come back here again . . .

She goes. Nick doesn't move, it's as if all the life has drained out of him. After a moment Emily comes stomping back in. She's forgotten her cap.

You're a lousy fucking shag an' all.

She stomps out again. Nick goes behind the counter and brings out a bulging hold-all, which he puts on a table and starts to rummage through it, taking out clothes etc. He finds his Building Society book, which has a wad of twenty pound notes sticking out of it. He counts the money. Pasha appears in the house doorway. Nick turns.

Nick Alright.

Pasha Where's George?

Nick George . . .

Pasha You remember George.

Nick Out, I don't know, I only just got here. I thought he was with you.

Pasha I thought he was here.

Pasha turns back into the house.

Nick (*can't resist a dig*) I'm gonna miss our little chats.

Pasha Nick, I've got two words to say to you, and they're not 'let's dance'.

Pasha walks back into the kitchen, almost bumping into George coming the other way.

Where are you going?

George I want to talk to him.

Pasha Have you done it yet?

George Can we talk about it later –

Pasha George, have you done it yet? Have you made the call?

George It – look, I've been thinking about it and –

Pasha There isn't much time, I thought we'd agreed.

George He's my *brother*.

Pasha (*trying to be patient*) But this is what we talked about. You said –

George (*almost in tears*) *You* said it was my decision!

George breaks away and walks to the door to the shop. Pasha watches him for a moment, then turns and goes upstairs. Nick looks up. Pause.

Alright.

Nick Alright.

George You off out?

Nick In a sec, someone's picking me up.

George You gonna be long? Mum had a bad day, I said I'd tidy up. She got a bit tired and put chutney in the till again.

Nick Go ahead.

George What's the bag for?

Nick I've, um, decided to go away for a bit.

George Where?

Nick I don't know yet. Long way away. Start again, somewhere nobody knows me. Back of beyond. Out in the sticks. Maybe Taunton.

George Taunton?

Nick There's a situation here . . . I can't explain.

George When?

Nick Tomorrow, first thing. There's something I've got to do tonight, it's . . . I can't get out of it.

George What about us?

Nick 'Us'.

George Your family.

Nick (*stuffing the clothes and money back into the bag*)
George, I haven't been in this family for years.

George Whose fault's that?

Nick You see! There we go again! 'What–Nick–Did'!

George I didn't mean it like that. You was the one
always rowing with Mum and Dad and Pasha, you was
the one who nicked the car.

Nick No, George! When that copper brought me back
to the house I thought something great was gonna
happen. It was a chance, do you see what I mean? It was
a chance for us all to start again. It sounds so stupid
now, I thought we was all going to be proud of each
other. I thought if I could hold up my hands to what
I did, then they would do the same. But I was wrong.
Nothing happened.

George What's that got to do with Emily?

Nick You don't understand . . .

George Why, Nick?

Nick looks at George, he doesn't know what to say.

Nick . . . Because no one ever gave me the strength to
say no . . .

George That's not good enough, Nick. *I* did it, *I* said no.

Nick What are you talking about?

George I know where you're going tonight, what you're
going to do.

Nick How – ? Pasha . . .

George When he told me I was so tempted – after everything you've done, it would have been so easy, just one phone call . . . But I didn't do it. I said no. What's happened to you? I don't just mean Emily, I mean tonight . . . everything. You could get caught . . . you could get killed. All so's you can buy a car and get to London?

Nick (*shrugs, helpless*) . . . It's all I know . . . It's all I know . . . There's this line in the sand, and it's so thin you can hardly see it. And all you have to do is make the smallest of moves and you're there. And everything you've seen, all those cars and women and clothes, they're yours. It's such a tiny exchange, it's such an easy deal and there's nothing on this side holding me back.

George Is that all we are? 'Nothing'?

Pause.

It was all for you. Everything I did.

Nick I never asked you for that.

George . . . You're my brother. . . . What else could I have done?

Offstage, upstairs, Mum's slurred and sleepy voice is heard singing the first few bars of 'Dark Eyes'.

I want you to take me with you.

Nick *What*?

George I want to come with you. I'm serious.

Nick . . . No, George –

George Why not?

Nick You've got school, your exams. We've had this conversation.

George I don't care about them.

Nick Well you should. No one in this family's ever had a chance like you've got.

George I wish people would stop telling me how *good* I am. 'The good son.' I hate it, I hate school, all the kids, it's horrible. I've stopped answering questions, it's not worth it. We came out of English and Melissa Bowen spat at me.

Nick But this is what I'm saying, get your exams and you'll be out of here in no time, you won't need me.

George You know that's not true! Without you it'll be just me and everything else.

Nick What about Mum?

George We don't owe her anything, you said yourself.

Nick And Pasha?

George (*looking away*) . . . He'll be alright.

Nick Oh come on, he'd be in pieces without you.

George *This place*, Nick.

Nick It – no. All this stuff with Emily, you're not thinking straight.

George Give me one good reason why I shouldn't come with you.

Nick I can give you a million! You're sixteen years old!

George So?

Nick We'll be broke after a day or so, things will be really tough, you're not the type – I mean you read *books*.

George The Malinoffs. The Brothers Grimm.

Nick That was just talk, it doesn't work that way.

George But I've thought it all through.

Nick What are we going to live on then? This is insane . . .

George We'll open a café!

Nick *Please* tell me you're joking.

George We could! I could do the bookwork, 'Nick's Place'.

Nick (*looks at his watch*) I haven't got time for this, I should be getting psyched up!

George We'll send money back, help them out –

Nick It's cold in Taunton.

George It's cold in our bathroom!

Nick Life's hard there. No pier, no Emily.

George I'll manage.

Nick No friends.

George I hate my friends.

Nick No women.

George . . . None?

Nick I swear, well-known fact. No women in Taunton.

George Well, what they do?

Nick Baaaaaa!

George You're joking!

Nick Serious!

They laugh, but George stops. Pause.

George No. I'm not letting you win. People like you always win. You're always looking for more and you

don't know what you have. I'm not gonna be tongue-tied
with you any more. I want you to take me with you. If
you don't, if you go without me, I'll just get the next
train and come and find you.

Nick George –

George You can't do this, Nick, you can't leave me in
the middle of the very thing you want to leave. You can't
let my last memory of you be *this*. Besides. How will you
manage on your own? On the run. You're useless. I'm
forever finding your keys and wallet. You're right, there's
a million reasons why not. But I've never asked you for
anything. I'm asking you for this.

Nick . . . I'll be getting up really early.

George I'm up at five-thirty, I've got to pay the milkman.

*George stares at Nick imploringly. Pause. Nick shakes
his head in disbelief.*

Nick First sign of any trouble, I'm sending you home.

George (*ecstatic*) You won't know I'm there!

Nick I'm serious, George, we've got a lot of ground to
cover, I don't want you moaning 'cos you can't see the
House of Eliott.

George As if I would!

Nick And don't go bringing all your books and shit. Just
clothes, some sturdy boots.

George I'll get packing straight away. One book: *The
Voyages of Odysseus*, it'll bring us luck. You won't
regret this Nick, I swear.

Nick I'm beginning to already . . .

George We'll be like the last of the Samurai, roaming
from town to town, righting wrongs.

Nick (*warning*) George.

George I know, I'm sorry, I'm getting excited, I just – we're getting out! Go on, give us your bag, I'll hide it in my room.

Nick Don't say anything to anyone. For God's sake don't tell Pasha.

George I shall take it to the grave.

   Nick keeps hold of the bag for a moment.

Nick I, er, I'd better warn you, your hooded top's in there.

George What?

Nick Saves you packing it –

George Oh cheers Nick, bloody hell!

Nick (*laughing*) You're getting it back, aren't you!

   Sound off of a car horn. Nick jumps.

They're here. Shit, they're here . . . This is it then. I'll, um, I'll see you later.

George (*horrified*) You're not still going, are you?

Nick I've got to.

George You could be killed!

Nick It's fine, the blokes I'm with are experts.

George Hide! I'll tell them you're not here –

Nick George, I know what I'm doing –

George You're ill or something –

Nick There's six hundred quid in it for me, if we're getting out we're gonna need every penny.

George But –

Nick Listen to me. Sometimes you just don't have a choice.

Nick starts toward the door.

George You will be careful won't you?

Nick Of course I will.

George You wouldn't leave me here. With Mum and the shop and Pasha's hands, you wouldn't leave me to deal with all of that, would you?

Nick Never. It's you and me, George, we're getting out.

George What an escape it'll be, they'll talk about it for years. 'The crowds roar as they step from the chains.' (*He laughs.*) The Houdini's!

Someone knocks on the shop door, Nick jumps again.

Nick Jesus!

George You alright?

Nick George . . .

Pasha has entered from the house. He stands in the doorway.

George What is it?

Pause. Nick and Pasha stare at each other. Another knock on the shop door.

Nick (*shouts*) I'm coming! (*to George*) Remember what I said.

Nick starts towards the door to the street.

George Nick . . . Be careful.

Nick I always am.

Nick opens the door and steps out into the darkness, his voice faltering slightly as he greets the figure waiting for him.

Alright . . .

Sound of a car driving off. George doesn't turn to face Pasha, he stays looking at the door through which Nick has exited.

George I've let you down.

Pasha As if you could ever do that.

George . . . I couldn't do it. . . . In the end I couldn't do it.

Pasha (*gently*) No.

George Muggins . . .

Pause.

Don't go yet. I've got to cash up, keep me company.

Pasha Of course.

George How was she?

Pasha So so. She was quite shaken up last night. Your little adventure.

George opens the till.

George Don't I know it. She thinks me and Nick are trying to kill her. Says not to bother as she doesn't have any money. You want some tea? Pasha?

Pasha Some water.

George I had to promise her two hundred times I wouldn't do it again.

Pasha No . . . I don't think you will.

George crosses back with the water. Pasha is dabbing his forehead.

George Here. You alright?

Pasha What? A little tired perhaps.

George Do you want a *drink* drink? I've got the till open.

Pasha No no, no need.

He tries to drink the water, and spills some down his front.

George What's wrong with you?

Pasha I'm fine, it's –

George You're shaking.

Pasha Really.

George Tell me . . . *Pasha.*

Pasha looks distracted around the café.

Pasha Tell you . . . yes . . . yes . . . I should. There is something I have to tell you first. Something you must understand.

George (*shrugs*) OK.

Pasha It's about when we left. I never told you what happened to us.

George What?

Pasha Emigration in Russia was an impossible process, designed to stop you. The interviews, rejections, applications, rejections, it goes on for months. And the money! Oh God, the tax, the redecoration of your apartments . . . We scrimped and saved and begged. Some days felt thirty hours long we worked so hard. Luckily we had our cousins who'd been smart and got out in the chaos after the war.

George Lydia and Sergei!

Pasha (*nodding*) Lydia and Sergei . . . They sent official invitations to join them in the West. So finally after a year, year and a half, we are given a departure date. The three of us to go together, and it's only two days away.

Long pause. Pasha is shivering.

Your parents hadn't received their final K.G.B. permission. You need four, you see. Without them you can't go, and if you try and get caught, bam! The bottom of the pile.

The departure date is getting closer. What are we to do? We rush to the immigration office and after five, six hours we are admitted. As soon as I saw the official, his eyes on Sophia, I could smell trouble. My heart began to race, my knees shook and I wanted to shout. The final form lay on the official's desk.

'Comrade Inspector,' said your father, 'if you would be so kind as to sign and stamp this form, my wife and I can leave tomorrow and begin our new lives.'

The official looked at the form. 'I'm sorry Comrade,' he said, 'but I don't see what you mean, there is no form.'

'Here, Comrade Inspector,' your father said, 'it is lying on your desk in front of you.'

The official pretended to look about on the desk. 'Comrade I fear you are mistaken, there is nothing here that relates to your application.' I almost laughed, it was like a game.

Your father was beginning to sweat. 'Please, Comrade Inspector, if you would be so kind as to look at where I am pointing you will see the form.' The official stood up, straightened his tunic and gestured to Sophia. 'Come with me for a moment, Comrade, and let us see if we can't sort this out somehow.'

Slowly she got to her feet and followed him through a door. And we didn't move. And we didn't call out. And we didn't jump up and say no.

Long pause.

When she came back into the room her skirt was dirty at the knees. It . . . Her mouth . . . She looked at me with a kind of terrible pure pain and surprise like her back had been broken. Her husband, not yet twenty-five, sitting in his chair as still as a tree. So humiliated. So frightened. And when she sat heavily beside him they didn't look at each other. The embarrassment and the cruelty poured on this woman, this child . . . I wanted to grab a gun and empty it into the official's mouth. To spit and tear his clothes. But I didn't. We sat staring ahead. And nobody moved. And nobody called out. And nobody jumped up and said no. 'Silly me,' the official said breathlessly, 'it was here all along.' I heard his pen scratch on the paper, and the click click click of his boots as he walked out of the room.

Pause.

I look at you and Nick sometimes, the people in the streets, in here, and I think of the people back home, back then, a ghost inside me stirs, and it staggers me, the difference between a man and a man. I have become decadent. I go to supermarkets, watch quiz shows, I even have a Walkman. I've forgotten how it feels to live in fear.

Pause. Pasha frowns, confused, and looks at his hands.

I feel as if I've jumped into another man's skin. These aren't my hands. To sacrifice so much. The humiliation . . . the work . . . To run from gangsters, only to find them at home. Even so, my own blood . . .? *Now* I choose to say no? *Now* I choose to jump?

George What is it?

Pasha Remember I said the past is the sea? Beautiful, dangerous and waiting. Well, now it has found me. And

I didn't even see it coming. (*He touches George's face.*) Look at us. What a pair we make.

George You're shaking . . .

Pasha I did it for you, George.

George Did what? I don't understand. (*George stares at Pasha. The realisation shudders through him.*) . . . You said it was my decision.

Pasha You are free now.

Voice Off Nikolai!

Pasha George.

> *Pasha makes a move toward George, who flinches away, out of his seat.*

George.

> *Again Pasha moves toward him. George recoils further away, almost to the other side of the café. Pasha's arms drop to his sides, helpless.*

. . . You'll live . . . We all live.

Voice Off Nikolai!

> *Blackout.*